SURVIVAL
TO
SOVEREIGNTY

SURVIVAL TO SOVEREIGNTY

The 7 Rhythms to Heal Your Body, Rewire Your Mind, and Live in Alignment

Mar Morabito

Published by Game Changer Publishing

Paperback ISBN: 978-1-968250-90-4
Hardcover ISBN: 978-1-968250-91-1
Digital ISBN: 978-1-968250-92-8

GC GAME CHANGER
PUBLISHING

www.GameChangerPublishing.com

To God—

The Source of my breath, my strength, and my story.

I was supposed to die. But You kept me here.

You knew the fire I would walk through. You knew the pain I would face.

But You also knew I would rise. Not for my glory, but for Yours.

You chose me not because I was perfect, but because I would never stop seeking the truth.

And You entrusted me with a message that could only be born through suffering, surrender, and unwavering faith.

This book exists because You never let go of me—even when I let go of myself.

To my family—

You were my anchor when I was lost at sea.

When I couldn't walk, you carried me.

When my mind broke and my body gave out, your love kept me tethered to life.

You reminded me of who I was—when I no longer recognized myself.

To my parents and sisters: you held the line. You loved me unconditionally through every version of myself.

To my nieces and nephew: before I ever fully understood who I was, you three saw me. You called me "Mar" before I had the strength to claim it. That name, that truth, it became the compass home.

God may have given me the battle,

But He appointed you as my army.

And for that, I am forever grateful.

Without you—none of this would exist.

With all my heart,

– **Mar**

Read This First

Thank you for buying and reading this book.
To support your journey, I've created a FREE Portal & Community
filled with tools, videos, and resources to keep you connected and
accountable as you integrate this work into your life.

Scan the QR Code below and use the password: book **to enter.**

SURVIVAL

TO

SOVEREIGNTY

THE **7 RHYTHMS** TO
HEAL YOUR BODY,
REWIRE YOUR MIND,
AND **LIVE** IN ALIGNMENT

MAR MORABITO

TABLE OF CONTENTS

PREFACE

ICU AND THE RUPTURED APPENDIX

On May 24, 2006, I woke up in an ICU bed.
I had suffered a traumatic brain injury after being tasered or stun-gunned, beaten, and left broken.
I have no memory of what happened, only the bruises, the blood, the searing pain in my head and spine, and my seventy-eight-pound lab, Caton, lying across my body, licking my face, willing me back to life.

Even in that moment, barely conscious, barely alive, I felt an unshakable knowing:
I was going to be okay. I just had to get up and get help.

I spent nine days in the ICU. Every day, the doctor would hand me a piece of paper and ask me to write something. And every day, later on, I was told by my family that I had written:
"Marisa Morabito is going home."

On the tenth day, I checked myself out against all medical advice, fiercely committed to healing. That was the first step.

And it was there that God revealed something miraculous to me. A gift even through the pain and suffering.

He knew I had to break to finally surrender.

I wasn't really fond of God back then.
We'll get into that later, but that moment was clearly His doing.
Because inside that hospital, He revealed His face to me.
And showed me the power we hold.

He gave me a glimpse. A vision.
I saw myself living with purpose and alignment, a version of me that was whole, strong, and free.

But it would take years of falling, failing, and facing myself to water that seed into reality.

When I was younger, I always knew I was different, not just in the obvious ways, but at a deeper level. I could feel I wasn't meant to walk the path of conformity.
And yet, like so many, I got pulled off course.

Addicted to food. Addicted to drugs. Addicted to alcohol.
Addicted to the highs and lows of life.
I chased comfort. I chased distraction. I gave my power away, moment by moment.

But it was food that became my secret crutch: socially acceptable, but emotionally destructive.
It numbed my emotions. It disconnected me from my body and my power.

Until I realized the power of my mind and, more importantly, the power of a made-up mind.

But real healing wasn't just about getting out of that hospital bed.
It came from reclaiming my mind, my body, and my spirit.

While lying in the ICU, I realized something profound:

Health is our greatest wealth.

No amount of money could buy my way out of that bed.
The only currency that mattered was **self-responsibility, discipline, and belief.**

Years later, that commitment would be tested again.

In 2023, I found myself dying again.
But this time, slowly, quietly, almost invisibly, as an infection from a ruptured appendix made itself known.

My body was shutting down. I was in extreme pain.
At first, I thought it was just my gallbladder, fatigue, stress, or a hard training block.
I had been fasting, eating clean, and running daily.

But something deeper was wrong. I felt it. I knew it. My metrics were showing it.
I wouldn't listen.

Even fasting wasn't working anymore. I couldn't run because it hurt too much.

Looking back, that health crisis revealed the deeper truth:
Healing is not a one-time decision. It's a daily practice.
It's choosing alignment over comfort over and over again.

The only thing that saved me?
My abdominal cavity and muscles were so tight that they formed a protective barrier, keeping the infection from spreading to my entire body.

Essentially, my lifestyle and musculoskeletal structure protected me.

Mindset.
Fasting.
Discipline.
Habits.

That's what this book is about:

Choosing the sovereign path—every single day.

Through the hardest moments, the awakening came:
Life is not about chasing money, success, external validation, or comfort.
It's about daily self-mastery, internally validating, and reclaiming your authentic self.
The one who is fully expressed. Fully alive. Fully aligned.

And that's what I want to teach you through this book and the workbook within.

INTRODUCTION

THE ROAD BACK TO ME

I spent years asking God, *Why did You make me like this?*

My whole life, I wanted to be a boy, not because I was confused, but because that's where I felt the most like myself. I hated wearing dresses. I just wanted to run around shirtless like the other boys. I loved sports, couldn't relate to most girls, and found joy in creating, solving problems, and finding ways to make money. That was my happy place. **Simple. Direct. Driven.**

It took me decades to realize that my life wasn't a tragedy, it was a journey of redemption.
That true peace would come not from choosing sides but from integrating my masculine and feminine energies.

Now, I no longer feel the need to fit into any box.
Instead, I've created space within myself to be whole, **strong and soft, focused and intuitive, logical and nurturing.**

The truth is, we can all find ourselves.
It's not about changing who you are; it's about sitting quietly and long enough with who you've always been. Without distractions. Without proving. Without performing.

I learned to tune out the noise of the world and listen to the quiet voice within. That's where alignment happens. That's where *home* is.

For years, I chased approval, drugs, alcohol, success, money, and everything the world told me to want. I hid behind addictions, perfectionism, and performance, all while pretending to be someone I wasn't.

Until I realized I was living a life that wasn't mine.

Most people are doing the same, walking someone else's path, chasing validation, stuck in loops, disconnected from their own power.

The Sovereign Stride is about stepping out of that noise and reclaiming the rhythm of your own life.

It's a return to the inner child, the one we've all lost but still long for.

You don't need another productivity hack or vision board.
You need to become the person who can *hold* the life you say you want.

This book is a guide to becoming that person, someone you love, admire, and respect.
This isn't about chasing success.
It's about mastering you first.

Becoming the most authentic version of yourself.
The one who moves from inner alignment.
The one who doesn't flinch when storms come.
The one who commands peace, power, and presence without needing to prove anything.

This is a journey of self-mastery, where every step you take is a conscious choice to align with your highest self. It's about rewiring your mind and owning your life by taking full responsibility for who you are and who you are becoming.

"Sovereign" means claiming full authority over your life.
"Stride" means moving forward with strength, rhythm, and purpose.

Together, **the Sovereign Stride** means walking forward boldly and consistently, through whatever resistance life throws your way.

You don't need to become someone else.
You need to remember who you've always been.

Through seven deeply lived principles, I'll show you how I found my way back home and help you do the same.

This isn't about perfection. It's about remembering.
It's about rewriting the rules and walking forward in alignment with *you*.

THE 7 PRINCIPLES OF
THE SOVEREIGN STRIDE

1. Fasting & Time-Restricted Eating

- Master hunger to master yourself.
- Discipline begins in the body. Learn to control impulses and reclaim your power.

2. Prayer & Meditation

- Find power in stillness.
- Stillness is where clarity lives. It's how you connect with divine guidance beyond mental noise.

3. Sleep & Recovery

- Rest like it matters because it does.
- Regeneration isn't optional. True power requires cycles of rest, reflection, and reset.

4. Macronutrients & Nutrition

- Fuel with intention.

- What you eat shapes how you think, feel, and show up. Food becomes fuel for purpose, not pleasure.

5. Exercise & Movement

- Train the body to strengthen the mind.
- Movement isn't about fitness. It's a ritual of resilience, clarity, and momentum.

6. Communication & Relationships

- Build a deeper connection by being honest with yourself first.
- When you know who you are, your relationships become mirrors, not masks.

7. Goal Setting & Planning

- Turn vision into direction.
- A sovereign life is built with intention. Every action becomes an arrow aimed at your higher self.

This book is your compass.

Not to copy my path but to find your own.
This is not a book of fluff or shortcuts.
This is a soul manual for people ready to do the real work—the deep work—the *healing* work.

If you're done pretending, done performing, done hiding behind addictions and distractions, this book is for you.

I'm not perfect.
But I am aligned.
And that's the difference.

I didn't write this to impress you.
I wrote it to free you.

Walking the sovereign path will require you to do hard things.
To say yes to what you've always avoided.
To embrace discomfort.
To surrender the need for comfort and finally step into power.

Because everything you want lives on the other side of the resistance you've been avoiding.

So before we go on, I ask you:

What lights you up?
What makes you feel alive?

That answer?
That's your compass.
That's your purpose.

It's time to stop running.
It's time to start *walking*.

Who are you?

For me, "Mar" isn't just a nickname. It's an identity I had to *grow into*.

When my nieces and nephew first started calling me *Mar Mar*, it felt right, but I didn't know why. Eventually, it became just *Mar*.

I'm Italian. But in Latin and Spanish, the word *Mar* means "sea."
And the sea?
The sea doesn't ask for permission.
It *moves mountains.*
It *reshapes coastlines.*

It *destroys the false* and *rebirths the real*.

The sea can pull you under and still bring you back stronger. That's what life did to me.
I didn't drown. I *transformed*.
Over and over again, I came back.
Wiser. Bolder. Clearer. More whole.

When I shortened my name from Marisa to Mar, I thought I was choosing simplicity.
But what I was really doing was claiming my essence.
God didn't just give me a name—He gave me a frequency.
He buried a *message* in my identity that I had to suffer for, heal through, and *rise* to uncover.

Mar is a reminder.
That I am not here to be contained.
That I was never made to fit in.
That I *am* the current.
And I am here to flood the world with truth, sovereignty, and self-mastery.

This book is not just a message. It's a movement.
It's me becoming who I've always been.
And helping you do the same.

Are you ready?

CHAPTER 1

THE POWER OF A MADE-UP MIND

"Your thoughts have consequences so great that they create your reality."
– Dr. Joe Dispenza

The quote above shattered the old paradigm I was living in. It hit me so deeply because I knew it was true—I had lived the opposite for far too long. But once I began to grasp it, everything started to change.

The Moment of Awakening

I realized that our internal world—our thoughts, emotions, and beliefs—has the power to shape our external world. Thoughts are not just fleeting events in our minds. They are energetically potent signals that influence our behaviors, emotional states, and ultimately, the reality we experience.

Every thought triggers a chemical reaction in the brain, which produces a feeling. When repeated, these feelings create states of being. And over time, these states determine how we perceive the world and how the world responds to us.

If your thoughts are rooted in lack, fear, or unworthiness, your reality will reflect it. But if they stem from gratitude, abundance, and alignment, you will draw in clarity, growth, and fulfillment.

Where attention goes, energy flows. Repeating elevated thoughts and emotions doesn't just shift your mood—it magnetizes your future. Master your thoughts, and you master your life.

But my awakening didn't come through a divine download. It came through pain, survival, and surrender.

The War Within

The real battleground wasn't in a journal or meditation cushion. It was inside my own mind.

I was labeled with bipolar disorder, anorexia, bulimia, and multiple personality disorder. I was drowning in pharmaceuticals, bouncing between manic highs and depressive lows. My identity was swallowed by diagnoses.

I didn't just want to die. I was actively planning it.

I was exhausted. I wasn't sleeping. I was mixing pills, booze, drugs, and rage. That's how I ended up at Friends Asylum—a psychiatric hospital in Pennsylvania. And the second they took the shoelaces out of my shoes, I knew I was in trouble.

I walked through sterile white halls, the scent of disinfectant, body odor, and institutional food trapped in the air. The windows in my room were covered with thick, metal mesh. Escape wasn't even an option.

Patients in robes shuffled like ghosts. Some hooked to IVs. Blank stares. Drool at the corners of mouths. Tongue checks during med lines. Syringes jabbed in arms. No phone unless you've eaten your meal. No saying no to meds. The worst part? I didn't even think I was that f*cked up.

My family—out of love—put me there. But once I was in, it was no longer their decision. Insurance. Board approvals. Psychological clearance. I was trapped.

I remember calling my attorney from the hospital phone: "You have to get me out of here."

He tried. But it was a process. I was locked in a system that decided I was a threat to myself.

And in a way, I was. But not like that.

That experience changed me. Because for the first time, I saw where I was headed: a place where I would lose my voice, my freedom, and my soul.

It was my wake-up call. My mind wasn't just scattered—it was under attack.

And the only way out?
To take it back.

Rewiring the Mind

In 2006, I suffered a traumatic brain injury that nearly took my life. I remember the moment—a divine glimpse—where I felt God showing me: *"I'm not taking you home yet. There's more in you. You haven't tapped in."*

I didn't understand it then, but I do now. That was the moment He revealed to me the power of a made-up mind.

I didn't know then that I would one day train my mind to become unshakeable—that I would be so intentional with my thoughts and habits that I could rebuild a life of peace, power, and purpose from the inside out. But first, I had to stop outsourcing my power.

That meant getting control of my consumption: not just food, but thoughts, distractions, substances. I had been avoiding myself, numbing the noise, trying to fix internal chaos with external solutions. But everything shifted when I stopped running from myself and started sitting with myself.

This was the beginning of what I now call mental rewiring.

My Tools for Rewiring:

1. **Daily Journaling**
   Morning and night, I wrote my unfiltered thoughts. Then I asked:
   o   Is this belief true?
   o   Where did it come from?
   o   Does it serve my highest self?

2. **Thought Reframing**
   Circumstance → Thought → Feeling → Action → Result
   Old thought: *I'm not consistent.*
   New thought: *I'm becoming more consistent every day.*

3. **Meditation & Mindfulness**
   Observing thoughts without judgment. Using Dr. Joe Dispenza-style meditations to "leave the old self behind."

4. **Affirmation & Visualization**
   I visualized my future self and repeated affirmations until they became embedded in my identity.

5. **Environment Audit**
   I cut out what kept me stuck: people, media, and routines that reflected my old mindset.

6. **Emotional Rehearsal**
   I trained myself to feel joy, confidence, and abundance before they arrived.

7. Identity-Based Goal Setting

I didn't ask, *What do I want to do?*

I asked, *Who do I want to become?*

Biology and Belief

As I started rebuilding, I began to understand how deeply our mental patterns affect our biology. Science confirmed what my soul already knew.

Thoughts are electrical impulses.

Each thought fires a network of neurons. The more you repeat it, the stronger that circuit becomes. This is neuroplasticity—your brain's ability to rewire itself.

Emotions are chemical signals.

Thoughts trigger chemicals:

- Positive: Dopamine, oxytocin, serotonin
- Negative: Cortisol, adrenaline

Your nervous system responds to your mindset:

- Fight or Flight (sympathetic): triggered by fear, stress, overthinking
- Rest and Digest (parasympathetic): activated by gratitude, peace, love

Chronic stress equals poor sleep, weak immunity, aging, and inflammation. Gratitude and joy equal repair, hormonal balance, and resilience.

Your thoughts are not just "in your head." They shape your hormones, immunity, sleep, and even how fast you age.

Your consistent mental state becomes your biological state.

Data-Driven Discipline (WHOOP + HRV)

The deeper I went into self-mastery, the more I craved clarity.

That's when I discovered WHOOP and the power of tracking Heart Rate Variability.

HRV measures the space between heartbeats.

- High HRV = a resilient, recovered body.
- Low HRV = inflammation, stress, or poor recovery.

I began tracking everything:

- Fasting windows
- Foods
- Cold exposure
- Workouts
- Supplements
- Emotional state

And over years of data, the truth became undeniable:

Plant-based ketogenic meals + fasting = high HRV (110+)
Heavy carbs, processed foods, and animal-based meals = low HRV

WHOOP became my mirror. It showed me how my emotions, discipline, and choices shaped my recovery.

What gets measured gets mastered.

Fasting: My Path to Power

Fasting wasn't just about food. It became my weapon.

It taught me:

- To delay gratification
- To sit with discomfort
- To feel instead of being numb

Each fast was a mirror. It revealed who I was beneath the noise. It showed me my patterns, my pain, and my potential.

That's when I birthed my non-negotiables:

- Prayer
- Running & Training
- Time Restricted Eating
- Gratitude

Doing them daily—no matter how I felt—rebuilt trust in myself.

And the biggest breakthrough?

Fasting stripped away the noise so I could hear the whisper of God.

It wasn't about deprivation. It was about devotion.

The Spiritual Shift

I had known of God for years, but didn't trust Him.

Why would I? I had been told my sexuality made me wrong. That I was unworthy.

But I chose to seek Him for myself. I opened the Bible. I read it cover to cover.

And here's what I found:

- We are all sinners. (Romans 3:23)

- Yet God is love. (1 John 4:8)
- And nothing can separate us from His love. (Romans 8:38-39)

God didn't make a mistake when He made me. He made me fall in love on purpose.

And when I fasted with spiritual intention, I saw clearly:

The first temptation wasn't violence. It was an appetite. Satan controls people through cravings.

Even Jesus fasted for forty days before beginning his ministry.

> *"Man shall not live on bread alone, but on every word that comes from the mouth of God."* (Matthew 4:4)

Fasting became a spiritual weapon. It wasn't just about food. It was about alignment.

Your Turn: Activation

Awareness—Your Thoughts Create Your Reality

- What three limiting beliefs have been shaping your life?
- What three new beliefs will you choose instead?

The War Within

- Describe a time when your mind was a battlefield. What triggered it?
- Replace one lie with one truth.

Consumption Audit

- List what you're feeding your mind, body, and spirit.
- Which area needs the biggest shift?

Birth Your Non-Negotiables

- Name three things you will do daily, no matter how you feel.

Fasting for Freedom

- Where are you using food or distraction to numb?
- Try a twelve-hour fast. What comes up?

Spiritual Reconnection

- Reflect on Romans 8:38-39 and Psalm 139:13-14.
- Write a raw note surrendering old beliefs.

Your Made-Up Mind Declaration

"I have made up my mind to _____."

Closing Affirmation:

"I choose today to stop running and start rising. My mind is made up. My awakening starts now."

Let's begin. Not tomorrow. Not someday. Now.

CHAPTER 2

FASTING & TIME-RESTRICTED EATING

"Hunger is the teacher."
– Dr. Jason Fung

This one sentence shook me to my core. It forced me to see the truth I had been avoiding for years. **Fasting is the gateway to sovereignty.** When you stop reaching for the next bite, you finally start hearing your highest self. Food isn't just fuel—it's feedback.

Hunger doesn't just test your body—it trains your mind. It teaches lessons no book, no podcast, no coach ever could. It forces you to confront every part of yourself you've tried to outrun. The cravings, the emotions, the triggers. All of it.

And if you're willing to stay with it, something incredible happens: You gain real, grounded, unwavering power.

Because hunger is primal. It's wired into survival. And when you learn to regulate that primal drive without suppressing it or fearing it, you begin mastering yourself at the deepest cellular level.

My Addiction Wasn't What You'd Expect

I wasn't strung out in an alley, but I was enslaved by food, by validation, by constant dopamine hits. My drug of choice wasn't heroin—it was numbing. It was late-night binges followed by days of starvation. It was swinging between control and chaos, praise and punishment, obsession and shame.

I used food to disappear. To feel safe. To punish. To reward. It was how I coped, how I escaped, how I created the illusion of control. And beneath it all was a terrified girl who didn't know how to sit with herself.

I masked it as discipline, but it was desperation. Every fast I started was just a setup for the next fall. I wasn't fasting for clarity—I was fasting for control. But eventually, I broke. Again and again.

It wasn't until I hit that final wall—emotionally, physically, spiritually—that I realized I had to stop using fasting as a weapon against myself and start using it as a path back to myself.

I had to turn the very thing that once destroyed me into my spiritual training ground.

That's when everything changed.

The Breakthrough Fast

One morning, after a weekend of spiraling—binging, hiding, purging—I felt the shift. I woke up, looked in the mirror, and saw the aftermath of another war with myself. Puffy eyes. Bloating. Shame pulsing in my skin.

But instead of self-hatred, something different rose up in me.

"I'm done," I whispered, not in defeat, but in power.

That day, I started a twenty-four-hour fast. Not to punish myself, but to pause.

I told God, "This time, I'm not running. I'm not controlling. I'm listening."

And I did.

Hour by hour, I sat with every urge. I journaled every thought. I cried, I prayed, I walked, I breathed. And I began to understand that hunger was never the enemy. It was an invitation.

The discomfort wasn't something to fix—it was something to feel.

That one fast became a turning point. Because I didn't just abstain—I awakened.

What Fasting Gave Me

Fasting gave me back my power. Not because I skipped meals. But because I stopped avoiding myself. I started to see hunger as holy—a space where I could meet God, meet myself, and face what was underneath all the noise.

I began to feel the difference between emotional hunger and physical hunger.

I learned to ride the wave instead of reacting to it.

I discovered that the craving often had nothing to do with food.

And over time, the girl who once needed to control everything started trusting herself. The girl who once punished her body started listening to it. The girl who once hated hunger began to see it as her daily teacher.

Fasting taught me:

- To delay gratification
- To regulate my nervous system

- To break compulsive patterns
- To release emotional attachments
- To hear the still, small voice within me

It became my spiritual battleground—and my victory over myself each time I fasted.

Why Most People Don't Understand This

Most people think fasting is about weight loss. That's the least interesting thing it does.

Fasting is about energetic clarity. About emotional sovereignty. About spiritual resilience.

It's about stepping out of the noise of consumption and entering the silence where truth lives.

When you stop feeding your distractions, you start facing your truth.

That's where the magic happens. That's where the transformation begins.

And that's why I'll never stop fasting.

Not because I need to be skinny. But because I want to be free.

The Addiction Beneath the Appetite

What most people call "bad habits"—the endless snacking, the dopamine loops, the cravings—I saw as a doorway.

Every craving was a coded message from my nervous system.

I wasn't hungry, I was anxious. I wasn't starving; I was overwhelmed. And every time I reached for food when I wasn't truly hungry, I was choosing distraction over depth.

Fasting cracked that open.

It exposed the places I hadn't yet healed. The trauma. Overstimulation. The lies I told myself, like *I just need a little something.*

No—I needed to listen.

Once I did, I saw clearly: My hunger wasn't a problem. It was a compass.

That's when fasting became holy.

Not restrictive. Not performative. Not obsessive.

Sacred.

Because every time I sat through the urge and stayed, I became someone new.

I knew this wasn't a hack. This was a spiritual initiation.

The Cellular Awakening: How Fasting Rebuilt My Mitochondria and Changed My Life

Fasting didn't just change how I looked.
It didn't just change my mind or my emotions. It changed me on a cellular level.

It changed my mitochondria and my energy levels, which directly transformed my life.

I was able to observe this data in real time for seven-plus years with my WHOOP metrics and daily strains.

When you fast—especially when you practice time-restricted eating consistently—something incredible happens inside you. Your body initiates a natural process called autophagy, meaning "self-eating," where it begins cleaning out damaged cells, repairing DNA, and recycling old cellular material.

But even deeper than that, your mitochondria—the tiny power plants inside every one of your cells—start to evolve.

Mitochondria are responsible for producing ATP, the energy that fuels everything you do.

When you fast, you force your body to become more metabolically flexible, switching from using sugars (glucose) to using fats (ketones) for fuel.

And this shift does something miraculous:

- It increases mitochondrial biogenesis, meaning you literally grow new, more efficient mitochondria.
- It upgrades the strength and output of your existing mitochondria.
- It enhances your cells' ability to produce cleaner, longer-lasting energy.

In simple terms?

You don't just get leaner—you become an entirely different, higher-functioning organism.

The Proof in My Body and My Data

I didn't just *feel* these changes—I saw them, week after week, documented clearly through my WHOOP journal and recovery scores.

When I was strict with my time-restricted eating window and kept my carbohydrate intake very low, my mitochondria thrived, and it showed up instantly in my athletic performance.

My running heart zones shifted upward naturally. I would operate comfortably in Zone 4 (high aerobic) and often touch Zone 5 (anaerobic)—even on brutally hot SWFL days, even with a ten-pound weighted vest on my back, even running six or seven miles without crashing. My body was callused, not just mentally but cellularly.

I was built to endure because my mitochondria had adapted to become more powerful, more efficient, and more resilient.

But there was another side to this, and I could see it the moment I broke my time-restricted eating window, consumed too many carbohydrates, or consumed more animals than plants.

Everything changed.

I saw it immediately in my training data. My runs would no longer live in Zone 4 or 5. Instead, I would hover lower—in Zones 2 and 3—signaling a loss of mitochondrial efficiency and metabolic flexibility. I would feel heavier, slower to recover, mentally less sharp, and WHOOP would confirm it with a lower recovery score, decreased HRV, and elevated resting heart rate.

My running, once my sanctuary and strength test, became my daily diagnostic tool.
It told me, plain and simple, if I was living aligned with my optimal blueprint or not.

Why Tracking Matters

None of this would have been possible to fully understand without tracking.

Every day, I journaled:

- My fasting and eating window.
- What I consumed.
- How long I fasted.
- How intense my runs were (WHOOP's strain score).
- What heart rate zones I lived in during workouts.
- Sleep quality.

- Recovery markers like HRV, resting heart rate, and respiratory rate.

Over time, my own life became my experiment.
I didn't need a textbook to tell me what was best—my body and my data told me everything I needed to know.

The Cellular Truth

Fasting made me not just mentally tough—it made me *cellularly armored*.
The stronger my mitochondria became, the stronger my spirit became.

And the beauty is:
This transformation is available to anyone willing to live in alignment with their biology, instead of against it.

If you're serious about your performance, your longevity, and your resilience, you must master mitochondrial health.
You must listen to what your body is telling you and verify it with real data.

Because when you live like this, you become undeniable—not just in mind, but in body and spirit.

The truth is, we are domesticated animals living in an overstimulated world. We were not designed to graze all day. We were designed to feast, fast, move, rest, and heal—in rhythm with nature.

Look at the wild: animals instinctively fast. They eat only when they need to. No DoorDash. No sugar cravings. No emotional eating.

They honor the cycles we have forgotten—and that forgetting is slowly killing us.

Here's the hard truth:
We created our sickness.
But because we created it, we also hold the power to heal it.

Fasting: Far More Than Weight Loss

Let's address the biggest lie first:

Fasting isn't about weight loss.
That's the least interesting thing it does.

Fasting rewires your relationship with yourself.
It teaches you:

- Delayed gratification
- Mental resilience
- Emotional regulation
- The art of non-reaction

It clears space—mentally, emotionally, spiritually—so you can finally hear what your body and soul have been trying to tell you all along.

There are two types of humans:

- **Sugar Burners**: Constantly feeding. Chasing the next hit. Crashing. Inflamed. Irritable. Disconnected.
- **Fat Burners**: Efficient. Clean-burning. Focused. Grounded. Metabolically flexible.

Most people have never experienced true ketosis—what it's like to run on their own fat stores with steady, powerful energy. But I have.

Not because I'm special.
Because my metabolism is trained.

This isn't hype. It's not a guess.

It's backed by hard data.

When I follow a clean, whole foods diet and fast daily, my WHOOP data shows:

- Higher HRV
- Better recovery
- Lower inflammation
- Deeper sleep

I train hard. I don't break down.
I build.

This is the art of knowing oneself.

It's not a coincidence.
It's not luck.
It's alignment.
It's awareness.
It's self-mastery.

We are both the problem and the solution.
The faster you own that, the faster you evolve.

Fasting: My Chosen Battlefield

Fasting is where I train.
It's where I sharpen.
It's where I remember who I am.

If I can master my response to hunger—the most primal instinct we have—I can master anything.

This isn't about abs.
It's about reclaiming your mind, power, and control. Renewing your cells on a cellular level.

Triggering Mitochondrial Biogenesis. Fasting signals your body to create *new* mitochondria through a process called *mitochondrial biogenesis*. This is your body adapting to lower energy availability by upgrading its internal energy systems.

Removing Damaged Mitochondria (Mitophagy). Just like autophagy clears out cellular junk, mitophagy clears out old, dysfunctional mitochondria. This keeps your energy systems clean, efficient, and resilient.

Enhancing Mitochondrial Efficiency. In a fasted state, your cells learn to produce energy (ATP) more efficiently and with less oxidative stress. You shift from burning sugar (glucose) to burning fat (ketones), which is a cleaner fuel.

Reducing Inflammation and Oxidative Damage. Fewer damaged mitochondria equals less free radical production. This lowers inflammation and supports better recovery, longevity, and cognitive clarity.

Your body? It's just the reflection of that inner decision.

Your physical form mirrors your self-talk, discipline, emotional maturity, and spiritual strength.

Reflection Questions: Pause Here

Take a moment.
Ask yourself:

- *What is my relationship with hunger—do I fear it, avoid it, or use it as a signal to go deeper?*
- *When was the last time I sat with a craving without acting on it? What surfaced?*
- *Am I eating to nourish my body, or to escape my feelings?*
- *What story have I been telling myself about food, control, and discipline?*

- *Do I believe I have the power to master my mind, or have I been outsourcing that power?*
- *What would it feel like to not be controlled by impulses—to fully trust myself?*
- *Where in my life am I consuming more than I'm creating?*
- *What discomfort have I been avoiding that might actually be the doorway to my growth?*

Remember, fasting isn't about going without. It's about returning to yourself.

What Happens When You Stop Eating
The Real Science Behind the Fast

Before I understood fasting, I thought it was just "skipping meals."

I had no idea it was a biological and spiritual reset button.
A way to allow my body to heal, repair, and realign without the constant chaos of digestion.

Here's what actually happens—hour by hour:

12 Hours: The Shift Begins

After twelve hours, your body finishes digesting its last meal.
You officially enter a **fasted state**.

- Insulin levels begin to drop.
- Your body taps into stored glucose (glycogen) for energy.

For beginners, a twelve-hour fast is a powerful start. Close the kitchen at 8 p.m. Open it again at 8 a.m. No midnight snacks. Just deep rest.

At twelve hours, you're not just skipping a meal—you're triggering metabolic switching.

Why It Matters:

- Your body starts to shift from sugar-burning to fat-burning.
- Insulin drops, unlocking fat stores.
- Blood sugar begins to regulate naturally.
- Mental clarity may start to flicker in.

This is the foundation.
Gentle. Sustainable.
And you'll feel it.

24 Hours: The Reset Deepens

At twenty-four hours, glycogen stores are depleted.
Your body shifts deeper into fat-burning mode, entering **ketosis.**

Now, ketones—not glucose—become your primary energy source.

Ketones are clean fuel.
No blood sugar crashes. No brain fog.
Just sharpness, steadiness, and surprising energy.

Even more:
Autophagy begins—your body's self-cleaning system.

Damaged cells? Old proteins? Junk DNA?
Your body starts recycling them into building blocks for healing and renewal.

Why Autophagy Matters:

- Clears out broken cells linked to disease.
- Reduces the risk of Alzheimer's, cancer, and autoimmune issues.
- Strengthens tissue repair.

I see autophagy as spiritual, too:
God is clearing out the old to make space for the new.

Emotionally, this is where things rise.
Without food to numb you—you feel it all—and healing begins.

36 Hours: Growth Hormone Spikes

At thirty-six hours:

- Insulin is extremely low.
- Growth hormone surges up to five times the baseline.

You're burning fat efficiently.
You're preserving lean muscle.
You're optimizing recovery.

Growth Hormone Benefits:

- Fat burning increases.
- Muscle tissue is protected and repaired.
- Skin, joints, and bones strengthen.

This is when fasting becomes undeniable.

Energy feels clean and limitless. Mental clarity becomes profound. Emotional strength deepens.

At this point, it's no longer just a physical fast.
It's a spiritual awakening.

48 Hours: Inflammation Drops, Stem Cells Activate

Two days without food. Here's what's happening:

- Inflammation plummets.

- The immune system resets.
- Stem cells activate.

Your body isn't dying. It's rebuilding stronger, cleaner, and faster.

If you struggle with autoimmune conditions, gut problems, or hormonal imbalances, this is where deep healing starts.

Hunger now feels different, too. It's not panic. It's peace.

You're clear. You're steady. You're fully present.

And you realize:
You are far stronger than your cravings.

Your body isn't just *surviving* without food—it's rebuilding. Your hunger might come in waves, but it's different now. It's not a craving. It's a signal. And once you sit with it, you'll notice you're actually okay. You're *clear*. You're *present*. And that's where the real spiritual strength is developed.

Two full days without food. And your body doesn't hate you—it *thanks* you.

At forty-eight hours, inflammatory cytokines, the molecules that cause bloating, pain, and chronic illness, are dramatically reduced. Your body is calm. Focused. Clean.

Even better, stem cell production increases, particularly in your gut lining and immune system.

Why It Matters:

- Gut health equals brain health. This is your second brain.
- A healthier immune system equals fewer flare-ups, sickness, and fatigue.
- You're no longer feeding inflammation—you're extinguishing it.

This is where I reset to feel completely *in flow*. My joints feel amazing. My digestion is silent. My mood is grounded. My skin is glowing. I'm in my body, but not *bound* to it.

72 Hours: Full Regeneration

At seventy-two hours, your body reaches deep healing states:

- Complete autophagy.
- Stem cell regeneration of the gut lining, immune system, and even brain tissue.
- Insulin sensitivity is restored.
- Cravings dramatically reduce.

You're no longer ruled by your hunger—you're in charge of it. This is when I always feel like my body, mind, and spirit are finally on the *same page*. It's hard. It's humbling. But it's worth it.

This is the full reset. Not everyone needs to go this long, but this was where I truly met myself.

- The full autophagy cycle has been completed.
- Stem cells regenerate organs, skin, and immune cells.
- Cravings are gone, not from discipline, but from detox.
- Your body is in full repair and renewal mode.

Seventy-two-hour fasts leave me feeling like a new human. Not lighter in weight—lighter in *burden*.

The emotional freedom is just as real as the physical clarity. And spiritually, I'm always reminded that this body is a temple, not a trash can.

Time-Restricted Eating (TRE): The Daily Discipline

If extended fasts feel overwhelming, *don't stress*. The real power is in the *daily rhythm*.

Time-restricted eating is simply choosing a window—twelve, fourteen, sixteen hours—during which you fast, and during the rest, you eat. That could look like eating from 12–8 p.m. (16:8), or even 10 a.m. to 6 p.m. (14:10).

Why it works:

- Insulin spikes are reduced.
- Your digestive system takes a daily break.
- Your eating becomes aligned with your circadian rhythm, which boosts your metabolism and hormone balance.

It's like training your body to expect food at certain times, not all the time. You're no longer living in a reactive state. You're leading yourself.

The Key: Start Where You Are

Don't feel like you have to do a seventy-two-hour fast tomorrow. Maybe your first step is:

- Closing your kitchen after dinner.
- Drinking more water.
- Tracking how you feel after twelve hours fasted.
- Breaking your fast with nutrient-dense food, not junk.

This isn't about restriction. It's about reclaiming your energy, your focus, your clarity—*yourself.*

Ask Yourself:

- *What's one small window I could close to create more alignment in my day?*

- *Am I eating because I'm hungry or because I'm emotionally unsettled?*
- *When do I feel my best? How can I create more of that state?*
- *What would happen if I trusted my body instead of fearing hunger?*

Fasting isn't about punishment.
It's about healing.
It's about discipline.
It's about listening.
And for me, it's about God.

It's how I return to center and remind myself that I am not a slave to my cravings and emotions. I am a child of the King. And I choose to be in alignment with my most unapologetically authentic self.

The Daily Warrior Practice

You don't have to fast for three days to transform. The real power comes from *consistency*, and that's where TRE comes in.

Time-restricted eating means choosing a daily window to eat and sticking to it.

Most common protocols:

- **12:12**: Eat from 8 a.m. to 8 p.m. (great starting point).
- **14:10**: Eat from 10 a.m. to 8 p.m. (adds deeper benefits).
- **16:8**: Eat from 12–8 p.m. (entry-level rhythm).
- **18:6** Eat from 12–6 p.m. (the gold standard for metabolic health).
- **20:4**: 2-6 p.m., or 1-5 p.m. (advanced fat-burning protocol—warrior fast).
- **OMAD** (One Meal A Day) 22:2 or 23:1 (metabolically elite)
    - **22:2** Eat between 4 p.m. and 6 p.m.
    - **23:1** Eat a single meal, typically between 5 p.m. and 6 p.m.

Benefits of TRE:

- Keeps insulin low and stable.
- Boosts energy and focus in the morning.
- Gives your body time to fully digest and detox overnight.
- Builds discipline, structure, and rhythm in your day.

When your body knows when to expect food—and when not to—everything regulates. Hunger. Hormones. Energy. Emotions.

TRE taught me how to lead myself. Every single day I do it, I get a chance to say, "I trust myself. I don't need instant gratification. I choose alignment."

Final Word: Listen. Track. Honor.

Fasting is personal. Your body is wise. So ask it questions like:

- *How do I feel after eating this way?*
- *What triggers my cravings?*
- *Am I eating out of hunger or habit?*
- *What would it look like to actually feel good in my body?*

The goal isn't perfection—it's *awareness* and *alignment*. Some days I need more food or rest. Some days I go deeper and fast longer. But every day I show up with the same intention:

To be in charge of my life.
To feel aligned in my body.
To be led by truth, not appetite.
And to walk in the power God gave me.

You don't need more willpower. You need fewer distractions. Start with the next fast.

Reflection + Action Workbook for Fasting

Reflection Questions:

- *How did my body feel when I first began fasting?*
- *What emotional urges or triggers did I experience during my fast?*
- *What physical sensations did I feel when hunger hit? How did I respond to them?*
- *What positive changes did I notice in my body or mind (energy, clarity, calmness, etc.)?*
- *What limiting beliefs or fears surfaced during this fast?*
- *What do I feel most proud of completing this fast?*

Reflection + Action Workbook for Time-Restricted Eating (TRE)

Reflection Questions:

- *What is my current eating window?*
- *How do I feel at the start of my fasting window?*
- *How do I feel when I break my fast—physically, emotionally, mentally?*
- *What's been the hardest part about following a TRE window so far?*
- *What positive impacts have I noticed since starting TRE?*
- *What obstacles or cravings tend to show up, and how can I address them moving forward?*

Action Steps:

- **Choose your window.** Select a TRE window to start (e.g., 12:12). Set the time you begin and stop eating, and stick to it for the next seven days.
- **Start simple.** Begin with a manageable window—twelve hours of fasting can be a great entry point if you're new.

- **Focus on hydration.** Drink water, electrolytes, herbal teas, or black coffee during fasting hours. This will help you stay hydrated and curb hunger.
- **Plan your meals.** When your eating window opens, aim to eat nutrient-dense meals (e.g., protein, healthy fats, and fiber). Avoid processed foods.
- **Track your progress.** Keep a daily log of how you feel during fasting hours, your energy levels, and any emotional shifts.
- **Stay consistent.** Consistency is key to allowing your body to adapt to the fasting windows. Try sticking to the same window for seven days before adjusting.
- **Reflect weekly.** At the end of the week, review your feelings, cravings, and energy levels. Adjust your window as needed (e.g., increase fasting time if you're ready for more benefits).

Chapter Takeaway:

- Addiction shows up in many forms, not just substances.
- Fasting reveals emotional dependencies and teaches self-control.
- The power of choice is reclaimed when you master hunger.
- True transformation requires confronting your discomfort.
- Spiritual wisdom often uses fasting as a method of breakthrough.

Challenge: Spend a minimum of twelve hours without food and journal every emotional or mental urge to eat. Don't focus on weight loss—focus on what the craving reveals.

CHAPTER 3

SLEEP & RECOVERY

"The shorter your sleep, the shorter your life."
– Dr. Matthew Walker

Sovereignty Begins with Sleep: Reclaiming the Night to Rule the Day

The Role of Sleep in Human Sovereignty

Sleep is the ultimate reset mechanism for the brain, hormones, metabolism, and mood.
Deep sleep clears emotional debris through REM processing, builds willpower, and helps the body *reset its relationship with dopamine*, the chemical of desire.

Every night, we are given the chance to heal. To release the body's burdens. To recover not just physically, but emotionally and spiritually. Sleep is not just passive—it is a divine recovery mechanism gifted to us daily. Sovereignty starts when we honor that sacred time.

Sovereignty over our impulses *starts* with reclaiming our night's sleep.

What I didn't know until looking back and connecting the dots is that my poor sleep fueled my addiction.

"Every night we skip sleep is like pulling an all-nighter on our mental, emotional, and metabolic stability."

Sleep deprivation is the silent saboteur—more dangerous than any craving, more destabilizing than any trigger. When I don't get proper rest, I already know I've rigged the game against myself. My margin for error shrinks. My mood tightens like a wire. My hunger spirals.

The clarity that usually anchors me starts slipping, and that's when the cravings creep in. Food becomes comfort. Emotions become louder. Reactions become sharper. And suddenly I'm in a storm I didn't see coming, but one I created myself. I've learned that poor sleep is never just poor sleep—it's a domino that knocks everything else out of alignment: food, mood, focus, willpower, even identity. I become someone I don't want to be.

And that's the relapse pattern—where I've historically slipped, binged, or exploded emotionally. But now, I see it. I've become aware. Awareness is power. This is why I believe everyone should be wearing a WHOOP. It's not just a fitness tracker—it's a mirror. The data doesn't lie. When I wake up and see a red recovery, I don't judge it—I make a plan.

I know to expect a shorter fuse. I know my hunger might be louder. I know my clarity might be foggy. And because I know that, I can navigate it. I can pivot. I can heal in real-time. I can course-correct my rhythm. That's what it means to live in alignment—not to be perfect, but to be present enough to know what's unfolding before it derails you. Sleep is the foundation. Recovery is the rhythm. And without it, even the strongest version of me can be pulled back into survival mode. But with it, I become sovereign again.

So, let's take a deeper look at why it is important to get the proper sleep.

When our brains are sleep-deprived, it reduces inhibitory control, so we are less able to resist cravings, especially from sugar, alcohol, and other dopamine-triggering substances.

Lack of sleep causes dopamine dysregulation, which heightens the brain's reward system.

This causes us to be more vulnerable to pleasure-seeking behaviors to help us compensate for the fatigue we are feeling. Have you ever noticed this happen?

Ghrelin, the hunger hormone, increases along with cortisol when you aren't getting enough sleep, all while simultaneously decreasing your leptin, your satiety hormone.

If you are trying to lose weight and you aren't getting enough quality rapid eye movement sleep, also known as REM sleep, you are fighting a losing battle. You must fix your sleep before anything else will change.

In fact, you probably find yourself in a cycle of late-night binge eating and extremely poor food choices.

Let's explore the role of these hormones in sleep and in general.

Cortisol is a steroid hormone produced by your adrenal glands in response to stress and as part of your body's natural circadian rhythm. It's often labeled the "stress hormone," but it's crucial for regulating sleep-wake cycles, energy, metabolism, and inflammation.

Our "Circadian Rhythm Anchor" is how I like to reference it because it naturally rises in the early morning, helping you wake up and feel alert, before gradually declining throughout the day and ideally, reaching its lowest point at night, allowing melatonin, the sleep hormone, to take over and help you fall asleep.

Stress and cortisol disruption happen with chronic stress or poor lifestyle habits, which causes elevated nighttime cortisol, which then leads to difficulty falling asleep, frequent waking during the night, poor sleep quality, reduced REM and deep sleep.

The other thing to be aware of is your cortisol levels and recovery. If cortisol levels stay too high, your body remains in a state of alert and doesn't fully shift into rest-and-repair mode, which is essential for recovery, hormonal balance, and cellular regeneration during sleep.

Tips to Support a Healthy Cortisol Rhythm:

- Wake up with sunlight exposure, ideally within thirty to sixty minutes of waking
- Avoid caffeine after 2 p.m.
- Reduce blue light exposure at night
- Eat balanced meals to avoid blood sugar crashes
- Practice wind-down routines (e.g., journaling, deep breathing, magnesium supplements)

The Deep Connection Between REM Sleep & Emotional Stability

Without REM sleep, emotional regulation plummets, again causing more impulsive, anxious, or depressed behavior and leading many to seek quick fixes via food or substances.

REM sleep is the phase of sleep where most emotional processing, dreaming, and memory integration happen. It typically occurs more in the second half of the night and is essential for emotional resilience.

When REM sleep is restricted (from stress, stimulants, alcohol, poor sleep habits, etc.), the emotional brain—especially the amygdala—becomes hyperactive, while the prefrontal cortex, your rational decision-making center, becomes underactive.

This imbalance creates a perfect storm for emotional volatility.

Let's take a deeper look at emotional regulation, stress management, cravings, and mood to understand how we feel with enough REM versus without enough REM sleep.

With healthy REM sleep, your emotional regulation responds calmly, and you think clearly. Your stress management and cortisol levels are balanced. Cravings and urges are within your control, and your mood is more upbeat and positive.

Without REM sleep, your emotional regulation is reactive, impulsive, or irrational. Your stress management levels are high, which spikes cortisol and increases anxiety. You are unable to resist the cravings and urges because you are seeking comfort in food, sugar, or substances.

Not getting enough sleep is a recipe for disaster. I have seen it play out in my life over and over again. I never used to sleep until I got my WHOOP seven years ago and realized how my metrics were off. Everything was harder when I didn't get sleep and easier when I did.

I was creating this spiral: **REM Sleep Loss → Emotional Reactivity → Coping Behaviors.**

What I found is that when I was deprived of REM sleep, my amygdala became hyperactive, leading to increased sensitivity to stress and perceived threats. It also lowered my prefrontal control and made it harder to self-regulate or delay gratification—something we need to do every day!

Negative emotions would rise. I was having more anxiety, my mood was low, and I was extremely frustrated, which led to coping and quick fixes like sugar, junk food, caffeine, alcohol, or drugs to numb or lift my mood. This then led to more disrupted sleep since these substances all degrade sleep quality, especially REM sleep. And thus, the cycle repeated itself.

I learned to protect my REM sleep because I know it directly affects how I feel emotionally.

How to Protect REM Sleep:

- **Go to bed and wake up at the same time each day.** REM builds in later cycles.
- **Limit alcohol.**
- **Avoid late caffeine.**
- **Reduce screen time at night.**
- **Wind down emotionally.** Journaling, stretching, and breathing lower stress before bed.

Signs You're Lacking REM Sleep:

- Waking up tired even after seven to eight hours of sleep.
- Mood swings or feeling emotionally "raw."
- Heightened sugar or carb cravings.
- Difficulty concentrating or processing emotions.
- Vivid dreams followed by abrupt waking.

Now, let's go back to the other hormone, ghrelin, which is a hormone primarily produced in the stomach that stimulates appetite. Think of it as your body's natural "I'm hungry" signal—it rises before meals and drops after eating.

But here's the key: sleep heavily influences ghrelin levels.

Sleep deprivation equals elevated ghrelin.

When you don't get enough sleep, especially under six to seven hours, your body increases ghrelin production and decreases leptin.

This sets the stage for increased appetite, especially for carbs, sugar, and fatty foods; more frequent snacking or binge eating; greater difficulty with portion control; and weight gain and insulin resistance over time.

In fact, research shows that in sleep-restricted individuals, ghrelin levels increase by up to thirty percent, while leptin drops by fifteen to twenty percent. Sleep-deprived people eat an average of 300 to 500 more calories per day, often from junk food.

Even a single bad night can spike ghrelin and make you feel hungrier the next day, even if your body doesn't need more energy. Have you ever experienced this?

Lack of sleep not only boosts ghrelin but also impairs the prefrontal cortex, weakening your ability to say no to cravings. You lose self-control. This heightens emotional eating, especially when stressed or anxious, which poor sleep also worsens. You will also notice that you will burn fewer calories at rest because it slows your metabolism.

Another study in *Nature Communications* found that sleep deprivation increases amygdala reactivity by over sixty percent.

People with insomnia are five times more likely to develop depression and two times more likely to develop anxiety.

Why Addicts (Food or Substances) Often Have Disrupted Sleep

Many addicts consume substances to "calm down," but alcohol, weed, stimulants, and binge eating all impair deep sleep and REM cycles. When coming off substances, you often suffer *rebound insomnia*, leading to relapse.

Many addicts carry unresolved trauma that manifests at night—the subconscious tries to process it, but without safe sleep, healing stalls.

Most have circadian disruption due to late-night use, blue light, and erratic schedules, which all decouple natural sleep-wake rhythms, disrupting melatonin and reducing overall rest.

Sleep is the first step to healing. Before changing your diet, quitting a substance, or starting a new habit, fix your sleep. The sovereign path begins with surrender, and true surrender is unconscious, nightly, and sacred.

Sleep debt is real, and the body tracks it. When recovery is incomplete, it carries that strain into the next day, compounding inflammation, stress, and cravings. Over time, chronic sleep debt can mimic the physiological stress of overtraining or trauma.

Recovery isn't just physical—it's neurological, hormonal, emotional, and cellular.

Top Recovery Benefits of Sleep:

- Repairs damaged cells and tissues
- Balances hormones and neurotransmitters
- Clears toxins and emotional "baggage" from the brain
- Builds emotional resilience through REM
- Enhances HRV and parasympathetic activity
- Regulates metabolism and energy
- Boosts immunity
- Unlocks neuroplasticity

Actionable Framework: "SLEEP SOVEREIGNTY"

S.L.E.E.P.

- Set a consistent bedtime.
- Limit screen time ninety minutes before bed.
- Engage in a nightly wind-down ritual.
- Eliminate late eating, especially sugar.
- Practice breathwork, prayer, or journaling to clear the mind.

Mini Workbook for Sleep Optimization
"Reset Your Sleep to Reset Your Life"

Know Your Sleep Hormones

- **Melatonin**: A sleep hormone that rises at night to help you fall asleep.
- **Cortisol**: A wake-up hormone that peaks in the morning and should drop at night.
- **Ghrelin**: A hunger hormone that rises with poor sleep, increasing cravings.
- **Leptin**: A satiety hormone that decreases with sleep loss.

Reflection:

Which one do you think is most out of balance in your body right now?

_____

Sleep Score Self-Assessment (Rate each of the following from 1–5:
(1 = Never true, 5 = Always true)

Statement	Score
I get 7–9 hours of sleep most nights.	____
I wake up feeling rested.	____
I fall asleep within 15–20 minutes.	____
I stay asleep throughout the night.	____
I don't rely on caffeine after 2 p.m.	____

Total Score: _____ / 25

Score 20+: You're likely sleeping well.
Score < 20: You have areas to optimize!

Create Your Sleep Ritual

Choose two to three of the following to implement tonight:

☐ Power down screens one hour before bed.

☐ Take magnesium glycinate or a calming tea.

☐ Journal three things you're grateful for.

☐ Do five to ten minutes of slow breathing/stretching.

☐ Avoid eating two to three hours before sleep.

☐ Go to bed by __p.m. and wake at __a.m.

Write out your wind-down ritual:

Identify Your Sleep Disruptors

Common culprits include:

- Scrolling on your phone before bed
- Stress or racing thoughts
- Alcohol or caffeine too late in the day
- Inconsistent sleep or wake times
- Overeating or eating too late

List your top two sleep disruptors:

1. _____

2. _____

What can you do to address each one this week?

1. _____

2. _____

7-Day Sleep Tracker

Day	Bedtime	Wake Time	Hours Slept	Energy on Wake (1–5)	Notes
Monday					
Tuesday					
Wednesday					
Thursday					
Friday					
Saturday					
Sunday					

CHAPTER 4

PRAYER & MEDITATION

"Prayer is when you talk to Me. Meditation is when you listen to Me."
– God

The Path to Stillness, Power, and Presence

There was a time when I believed power came from motion—hustling harder, running faster, doing more. But that belief nearly killed me. I was a workaholic who worked herself to the ICU.

Power doesn't come from motion.
It comes from presence.
It comes from stillness.

When I was in the ICU—barely alive, barely conscious—what saved me wasn't knowledge, discipline, or even the will to survive. It was stillness. A quiet knowing. A whisper of God in the silence.

It was the first time I truly heard Him.

Since then, prayer and meditation haven't been optional—they've been my oxygen. They weren't just part of my recovery; they were my *return*—to myself, to my spirit, to my source.

The First Opening

It wasn't a planned prayer. It wasn't in a place of worship. There was no pastor, no playlist, no journal prompt. It was just me…outside. A hoodie on. Darkness above me. The air was still. And I was tired—physically, emotionally, spiritually—worn out from holding everything in. I had come outside to write like I always did. Not because I had clarity. But because I didn't. I needed to get something off my chest and onto the page. I had no idea what was about to happen.

As I started scribbling, the words were jagged, messy, and frustrated. Thoughts blurred together. But the more I wrote, the more it began to feel like I wasn't writing to myself—I was writing *to Him*. The God I had screamed at. The God I had bargained with. The God I had run from and come crawling back to a thousand times. And as soon as I realized that, it hit.

Like a tidal wave. A full-body release. Tears poured down—real, raw, uncontrollable tears that I never let anyone else see. My chest cracked open. My jaw trembled. And for the first time in my life, I didn't feel *alone*. I wasn't journaling. I was praying. And I wasn't performing. I was being held. By a presence so tender, so vast, so real, that I stopped mid-sentence and just breathed.

And that's when I *knew*—this isn't about discipline or doing things right. This is about surrender. This is about showing up, even if it's messy—especially when it's messy. That was the first time I truly experienced what it means to be in communion. With God. With myself. With the pain. The pressure. The truth.

Since that night, everything has changed. Meditation became my grounding wire. The resistance didn't go away—but I stopped fighting it. I started seeing it as sacred. Because every breakdown is just an invitation to break open. And every time I do, He meets me again. Not always with a miracle. But always with peace. Not the kind you chase, but the kind that finds you when you finally stop running. In that moment, I realized something deeper:

Stillness Is the Portal

1. Resistance isn't the enemy. It's the teacher.
Every time I feel triggered, off, reactive, emotionally flooded—it's not random. It's not weakness. It's the moment my soul is asking me to *return*. Return to truth. Return to stillness. Return to the voice of my Creator. That's why I don't fight the resistance anymore. I face it. I pray through it because that's where the revelation lives.

2. Stillness isn't empty—it's full of answers.
The world is loud. Our minds are louder. But God doesn't yell. He whispers. And you can only hear Him when you get quiet enough. That's why my mornings and nights matter. That's why I journal. Why I scan my body. Why I get outside. Because stillness is where I reconnect with my inner compass.

3. Everything is spiritual.
Your food. Your relationships. Your relapses. Your wins. Your anger. Your love. It's all spiritual. Every day is a dialogue with the divine, whether you're conscious of it or not. When you begin to live this way, nothing is wasted— not even your darkest moments. They become the curriculum.

4. Devotion > Discipline.
I don't show up every day because I "have to." I show up because I *get to*. I've felt the difference between a day I pray and a day I don't. And I refuse to go back to living cut off from the Source that sustains me. This is why I meditate. Why I listen to my body. Why I breathe deeply, visualize light, and walk with intention. Because I *am* a vessel, and my peace is not optional—it's my weapon.

5. Your connection with God comes before your connection with anyone else.

When you learn how to sit with your Creator, you stop needing validation from the world. You stop projecting your emptiness onto others. You don't beg for love, approval, or answers. You already *have* them. Because you're not moving through life alone anymore. You're moving with God. And that changes everything.

Why We Avoid Stillness

Most people fear silence because they're afraid of what will surface when the noise stops.

But silence is the sacred doorway to healing.

In a world that rewards distraction, choosing stillness is revolutionary.

I chased chaos for years because it was familiar.

Food, addiction, pain—they kept me spinning just enough to avoid myself.

But every breakdown brought me back to the same truth: Everything I was looking for was already inside of me—I had just never been still long enough to listen.

Stillness isn't passive. It's the bravest thing you can do.

It is where strength comes from and is born.

You don't rebuild your strength in motion, you rebuild it in the pause.

Stillness is where you meet your truth without distraction.

It is where your nervous system exhales. Where your soul speaks without interruption.

We've been taught that *doing* more equals *being* more, but healing doesn't happen in hustle. Healing happens when you stop running and start resting in presence.

When you get still, the chaos doesn't win. You begin to hear the whispers beneath the noise: *You are safe now. You can let go. You are held.*

Let's be honest: stillness is terrifying.

It requires you to stop performing.
To stop numbing.
To stop avoiding the parts of yourself that you've buried under chaos, food, drugs, or distraction.

Most people avoid stillness not because they're lazy, but because they're scared.

Silence confronts you with what you've been running from.

I chased noise for years—externally with addiction, and internally with judgment. I thought if I moved fast enough, maybe I wouldn't have to feel the loneliness, shame, or confusion. I thought prayer was reserved for "good people," and meditation was too "woo-woo."

But silence, I've come to learn, is sacred.
And the moment you lean into it instead of away from it, you begin to heal.

Trading Performance for Presence

I used to perform spirituality like a to-do list—morning affirmations, gratitude journaling, a rushed prayer over my morning drink.

But presence isn't something that you check off a list. It's something you return to again and again.

It wasn't until life stripped everything away—my control, my strength, my plans—that I discovered presence wasn't something to do. It was something to become.

My Awakening to Prayer

Being gay, I felt rejected by religion.

I saw God as a judgmental figure—someone I had to hide from, not run toward.

But in the hospital, I ended up in the ICU after a trauma that left my left eye out of its socket, my spine and head bleeding, and my memory fractured. The aftermath of what law enforcement and my neurologist suspected was a brutal attack with blunt force, using a taser and or stun gun.

God didn't meet me with shame. He met me with love. Pure, undeniable, unconditional love. Prayer then became a channel, not a chore.

No conditions.
No doctrine.
Just presence.

And that's the gift.

Not a religion.

Not a ritual.

A relationship.

It doesn't require a perfect life. Just an open heart.

In that ICU bed, I felt cradled by something I couldn't explain but deeply remembered.

That moment cracked me open. And from that day forward, prayer stopped being about religion—it became a relationship. God became my friend, whom I could count on unconditionally.

Now, I pray like I breathe.
Sometimes I speak.
Sometimes I cry.
Sometimes, I sit in silence with my hand over my heart.
But it's always raw. Always honest.

Prayer, for me, is not about asking for things. It's about remembering who I am and *whose* I am.
It's returning to that unshakable truth: I am loved. I am guided. I am not alone.

Prayer is not about perfection—it's about presence.

Sometimes I kneel.
Sometimes I walk.
Sometimes, I speak out loud.
Other times, I just cry in silence.

And every single time, I feel God meet me where I am.

Not where I *should* be.
Where I *am*.

Sometimes, my prayers are words. Sometimes, they're tears. But they're always real.

What Meditation Taught Me

If prayer is my way of reaching out to God, meditation is my way of letting God reach me.

Meditation taught me to *listen*—to God, to my body, to the subtle wisdom within me.

It taught me that I am not my thoughts. I am the one witnessing them.

That realization changed everything.

Suddenly, I wasn't spiraling with every fear or trigger.
I could witness the storm without becoming it.
I could choose peace instead of panic.
Choice only exists in space, and meditation gave me that space.

Before I found stillness, I *was* my triggers.
I *was* my impulses.
I *was* my trauma responses.

But through meditation—daily, slowly, imperfectly—I started to gain space.
And in that space, I began to heal.

Meditation isn't about getting it right.
It's about showing up consistently.
It's about tuning into a different frequency—the one where God speaks in stillness.

Meditation helps me connect with myself and truly listen. It taught me how to stop reacting and how to observe my thoughts without being consumed by them.

When I sit in silence, I return to that place where I'm not my past, not my pain—I'm just here.

Alive. Awake. Aware.

Meditation is not about emptying your mind. It's about tuning into your soul's frequency.

Some of the practices that helped and still help me are breathwork, visualization, repeating a mantra or scripture, observing my thought patterns, and body scans (especially for trauma recovery).

Here's how I approach these practices:

- **Breathwork**: I do three to five minutes of deep belly breathing (inhale for four seconds, exhale for six seconds) to calm my nervous system.
- **Visualization**: I imagine God's light surrounding my body, flowing through me like a river of love.
- **Mantras/Scriptures**: I repeat verses like *"Be still and know that I am God"* or mantras like *"I am safe. I am loved. I am held."*
- **Body Scans**: Especially after stress or trauma triggers, I lie down and bring attention to each body part, noticing without judgment.

You Can't Be Sovereign Without Spiritual Anchoring

When your soul is disconnected, your discipline becomes dysfunctional.

You'll burn out chasing perfection when what you really need is *connection*.

Because sovereignty isn't about control—it's about *congruence*.
It's when your spirit, mind, and actions are aligned—not for applause, but for truth.

This Practice Matters—Every Single Day

You could be crushing your macros, fasting perfectly, and training like a beast—but without inner stillness, you're just spinning faster.

> *"You can't be sovereign if you're spiritually starved."*
> — *Mar Morabito*

You can't out-discipline a disconnected soul.

If you're not *anchored,* you're just performing.

Prayer and meditation *realign the compass.*
They help you *remember your why* before you chase your *how.*

They're not about being calm—they're about being *connected.*

To truth.
To presence.
To your higher self.
To God.

I've learned this over and over again:
You can't be sovereign if you're spiritually starved.

Stillness *realigns your compass.*

It reconnects you with your *why* before you run toward your *how.*

It allows you to notice what you've been avoiding so you can heal it instead of hiding from it.

Prayer and meditation keep the path sovereign by keeping the self-sovereign.

A Daily Ritual to Anchor Your Spirit

Here is a quick framework based on what I do daily.

Make it sacred. Make it yours.

Wake Up:

Place your hand on your heart. Breathe deeply.
Say: *"Thank you, God, for another day. I choose to walk in truth."*

Morning Prayer (10–15 minutes):

Talk to God like you would a best friend. No filter. No script. Just honesty. Ask for guidance. Express gratitude. Share your concerns, happiness, and fears.

Meditation (10–20 minutes):
Silence. Use breath, a mantra (*"I am loved," "I am safe," "Be still"*), or visualize God's presence surrounding you. You can also read a short scripture and reflect on it in silence.

Before Bed:

Light a candle. Take a breath. Ask yourself:

- *Where did I rush? Where did I pause?*
- *Did I speak to myself with love or judgment today?*
- *What fear did I feed? What truth did I honor?*
- *What do I need to release before I sleep?*

Let the day fall away. You don't have to carry it all into tomorrow.
You are safe to let go.

Then ask yourself:

- *Where did I stray from alignment today?*
- *Where did I choose truth over comfort?*
- *What can I surrender tonight?*

Let This Be Your Inner Sanctuary

The Sovereign Stride isn't just about what you *do*.
It's about who you *become* when no one's watching.

Prayer and meditation aren't tools to *fix* you.

They're spaces to *find* you.
And you, as you are—are already enough.

So be still.
And in the stillness, listen.
Your answers are not out there.

God is not far.
He is not in the noise.
He is not waiting for you to be perfect.
He is already here—in your breath, your silence, your stillness.

You don't have to find Him.
You only have to *stop running long enough to remember* that He never left.

He is within you, waiting.

CHAPTER 5

THE MEDICINE OF SOVEREIGNTY— MACRONUTRIENTS & METABOLIC ALIGNMENT

"Food was the first place I learned how to abandon myself, and the first place I learned to come home."
– Mar Morabito

Fuel with intention. What you eat shapes how you feel, think, and show up.

This isn't about nutrition. It is a spiritual framework. Every bite is either communion or confusion. Sacred fuel or self-abandonment. It is about discernment. What nourishes your purpose versus dulls your knowing. What keeps your antenna sharp versus clouds your divine whispers.

"The world worships taste, but the sovereign learns to worship Truth. And truth begins with what's on your plate." — Mar Morabito

Food becomes fuel for purpose, not pleasure.

"Food isn't like medicine. It is medicine."
— Dr. Mark Hyman

*"Food can be the most powerful form of medicine
or the slowest form of poison."*
— *Maria Emmerich*

When I came across these two quotes, something clicked. Not just intellectually, but in my spirit. They echoed what the *Sovereign Stride* is all about: returning to truth, to nature, to the inner compass that so many in this broken world have silenced.

For most of my life, food was something I either feared, manipulated, or misunderstood. I tried what culture told me to try. I measured macros. I restricted. I binged. I starved. I numbed. But when I read those quotes—when I saw food through the lens of *medicine*—something shifted. I began asking myself: What am I really feeding? My body? My soul? My ego? My emptiness?

That shift wasn't just philosophical. It was biological. Emotional. Spiritual.

I had been a vegan since 2007, but experimented with every diet on earth prior. But after my divorce, something shifted, and God revealed to me that I should shift my way of eating. I couldn't eat meat—it was never appetizing to me—but I could eat dairy and eggs. Still, something was off. My WHOOP metrics reflected it, and I didn't feel whole.

"When my HRV dropped after a meal, I stopped calling it 'coincidence.' I started calling it feedback." — *Mar Morabito*

"Metrics don't lie. My body was telling me the truth long before I was ready to listen." — *Mar Morabito*

After a 110-hour water fast, something shifted that I couldn't unsee.

I had cleaned myself out—not just in my gut, but on a *cellular* level. I could feel it in my bones. My skin. My spirit. The fog was gone. The noise was gone. And for the first time in months, I could hear my body speak with clarity.

You don't need this anymore, I thought to myself.

I looked at the eggs, the dairy, the leftover remnants of an animal-based food experiment I had convinced myself I *needed*. Post-divorce, post-collapse—I thought more protein, more calories, more "strength" was the answer. And maybe it did something for a moment. But it wasn't who I was.

I had forced animal products into my rhythm even when my soul resisted. I had watched my WHOOP metrics crash. I saw my HRV flatline. I felt the bloating. The breast tenderness. The hormonal symptoms every woman has been told are "normal."

But after that fast—after those 110 hours of total reset—I knew the truth:

Animal products do not align with me.

That day, I made the decision: I would return home to plants—but this time, through the sovereign lens of a *plant-based ketogenic lifestyle*. I wasn't just going back to veganism for the label—I was going back for *alignment*.

And over the next thirty days, my body confirmed everything.

My hormones stabilized. My sleep deepened. My moods leveled. I didn't feel bloated or inflamed. I didn't feel like I was riding some emotional rollercoaster built by estrogen dominance. I just felt...*clear*.

Women aren't meant to suffer.

We've normalized mood swings. Cramps. Breast tenderness. Skin breakouts. Bloating. But those aren't fixed realities—they're *feedback*. They're symptoms of internal chaos caused by what we're consuming.

I log my cycle, and WHOOP keeps track. I know when it's coming. But when I'm in full metabolic alignment—clean, fasted, and fueled by plant-based fats and protein—it arrives *seamlessly*. No mood drop. No warning signs. Just a sovereign body doing what it's designed to do—without resistance, without pain.

That was the moment I realized:

- I didn't need to fight my biology.
- I just needed to stop feeding it confusion.

And ever since I chose plants over animals—clarity over cravings—I've remained in alignment. Because when food starts becoming about *truth*, that's when the real healing begins.

When I leaned into a plant-based ketogenic approach, the kind of protocol that felt aligned with my spirit, that's when my HRV spiked. My recovery improved. My clarity sharpened. My emotional reactivity decreased. My performance ascended. I felt aligned.

Food is not just fuel—it is frequency. It is intelligence. And it's unique for every sovereign being.

What heals one may harm another. What brings clarity to one may cause confusion in someone else. The *Sovereign Stride* demands that we take full ownership of that—not outsourcing our nourishment to trends, influencers, or dogma, but instead, learning to listen to the wisdom written in our cells.

Because sovereignty begins with self-responsibility.
And food is one of the first battlegrounds where that responsibility is either claimed or surrendered.

Fuel with Intention

What you eat doesn't just affect your weight—it directly influences how you *think*, how you *feel*, how you *show up*, and how you *connect* to your purpose.

In this way, food becomes more than pleasure. It becomes fuel for purpose, a tool of intentional alignment. When you start to eat with clarity, your body becomes a vessel of energy, focus, and direction rather than one of distraction, sluggishness, and craving.

The Ketotarian Way: A Return to Divine Design

I fuel my body with intention by following a plant-based ketogenic lifestyle, often called *ketotarian*. This means I consume high amounts of healthy fats and proteins from non-animal sources while avoiding processed carbohydrates and sugars that disrupt my hormones, energy, and mental clarity.

This way of eating has not only helped me stabilize my hormones and reduce inflammation but has also given me mental clarity, spiritual attunement, and physical strength. I feel more connected to my highest self when I'm not weighed down by foods that dull my vibration or hijack my neurotransmitters.

This isn't just a diet—it's a spiritual return to how God originally designed us to eat.

"And the Lord God made all kinds of trees grow out of the ground—trees that were pleasing to the eye and good for food." (Genesis 2:9)

In the Garden of Eden, before sin and temptation entered the world, humans were sustained by the living plants and trees God created. We were given *every tree bearing fruit with seed in it*—that was our provision. Animals were not consumed. Life was sustained from the ground—vibrant, alive, and aligned with the rhythm of creation.

"Then God said, 'Behold, I have given you every plant yielding seed that is on the face of all the earth, and every tree with seed in its fruit. You shall have them for food.'" (Genesis 1:29)

It was only *after sin*, through disobedience in the Garden, that animals became part of the sacrificial system—their blood representing atonement, not sustenance.

Today, when I eat animal flesh, I feel the energetic and karmic weight of it. Animals often die in fear and pain, and I believe that fear becomes energy embedded in their tissues. When I consume that, I feel it. It clouds me. It lowers my frequency. I would rather consume *life*—foods that are alive, vibrant, full of enzymes and nutrients, and energetically clear.

Most of the foods I eat are raw or minimally altered, close to how they were created in nature. I eat for life force, not dopamine spikes.

Macronutrients: What You Eat Matters

Everything you consume falls into three main macronutrient categories:

1. Proteins
2. Fats
3. Carbohydrates

Each macronutrient carries a frequency—an intention. When understood and used wisely, they don't just build your body—they build your *capacity* to hold energy, to move through discomfort, to lead, and to heal.

Macronutrient Medicine: The Energetic Roles

Macronutrient	Purpose	Sovereign Effect
Protein	Structure & Repair	Builds resilience. Without it, you're brittle—emotionally and physically.
Fat	Clarity & Grounding	Fuels calm, stabilizes mood, and supports spiritual alignment.
Carbs	Energy & Danger	When conscious: support. When abused: sedate. Use with reverence.

Protein gives you structure. Not just in muscle, but in mindset. Without enough, you become emotionally brittle. I've noticed that when I'm protein-deficient, I don't just feel physically weak—I feel energetically porous. My boundaries blur. My confidence wanes. Protein provides the *backbone* of my biology and behavior.

Fat gives you steadiness. It grounds your nervous system. It gives your brain the fuel it was designed to run on. For a sovereign being, mental clarity is non-negotiable. I don't have time to be reactive. I can't afford brain fog. Ketogenic, fat-adapted living keeps me in a flow state where I respond—I don't overreact.

Carbs, when used intentionally, are tools. But when abused, they become chains. They flood your system with false comfort. They sedate you. Most people aren't addicted to food—they're addicted to *relief*. And carbs give that, but they rob clarity in the process. That's why I choose carbs that come from whole or living foods, fermented or raw sources—foods that support my microbiome, not enslave my mind.

Each plays a distinct role in how your body functions. But not all sources are equal. And not all combinations support your goals.

Protein: The Foundation

Protein is the most essential building block of your body. It repairs tissue, fuels muscle recovery, and is vital for hormone regulation, immune function, and cellular regeneration.

I live by a protein-forward philosophy—especially on a plant-based ketogenic path—because it's easy to under-eat protein when you're not conscious. That's why I intentionally supplement with things like Perfect Aminos and track my intake to ensure I'm giving my body what it needs to *build*, *repair*, and *thrive*.

Fats: The Fuel for the Brain

Healthy fats like avocado, olive oil, coconut oil, nuts, and seeds fuel ketosis, a state where your body burns fat instead of carbs. This switch supports brain clarity, reduces inflammation, stabilizes energy, and lowers the emotional volatility that often comes from blood sugar crashes.

When I'm in ketosis, fueled by clean plant-based fats, I feel clear, light, and centered. I don't ride emotional highs and lows. I stay in alignment.

Carbs: Be Conscious

Carbohydrates aren't inherently bad, but most modern carbs are processed, sugary, and inflammatory. They spike insulin, trigger cravings, and cause brain fog. I choose low-carb, living foods like fermented vegetables (sauerkraut and kimchi), cruciferous greens (cabbage and broccoli), and high-fiber options that nourish without inflaming.

Why It Matters

- **Calories in versus calories out matters, but *not all calories are equal.*** One hundred calories of sugar will hit your system differently than one hundred calories of raw nuts or protein.
- **Food either causes inflammation or reduces it**. There is no neutral ground. You're either eating toward healing or away from it.
- **Macronutrients shape your mood**. Low protein, unstable carbs, and bad fats lead to anxiety, depression, fatigue, and confusion.
- **You are not just feeding your body—you're feeding your brain, your hormones, and your spirit.**

The Sovereign Eating Framework
The Three Lenses I View Food Through:

1. **Biology**: *Does this nourish my body at a cellular level? Will it support muscle recovery, reduce inflammation, and stabilize hormones?*

2. **Energy:** *Does this give me sustainable fuel, or does it drain me? Will it raise or lower my vibration?*

3. **Alignment:** *Does this align with God's original design and my personal conviction? Am I eating from a place of love, presence, and clarity?*

If the answer is *no* to any of these, I pause. Because if food is medicine, then eating becomes a sacred act, not a mindless one.

Fuel for Your Calling

This isn't about restriction—it's about reverence.

When you eat with intention, you stop numbing and start *noticing*. You no longer chase energy—you *become energy*. You stop escaping your emotions with food, and you start using food to support the emotional clarity you're called to walk in.

You start eating in a way that aligns with who you're becoming, not the version of you that needs comfort.

You fuel like someone on a mission.
You eat like someone with a calling.
Because you are.

This is what it means to eat sovereignly.

You listen. You align. You let go of false comfort in favor of divine clarity.

You stop chasing food to fill a void and instead use food to fill your vessel with light, energy, and truth.

Because when your body is clear, your mind is calm. When your mind is calm, your spirit can speak.

And when your spirit speaks, your calling becomes undeniable.

Sovereign Reflection:
For the next three days, ask yourself before every meal:

- *What am I feeding—body, soul, or ego?*
- *Will this meal align me or numb me?*
- *Is this nourishment or noise?*

CHAPTER 6

COMMUNICATION & RELATIONSHIPS

"Real connection isn't built on lust. It's built on resonance. Knowing someone's not going to abandon your chaos, but sit in it with you until you find your breath again." – Mar Morabito

You must first master the relationship you have with yourself before any other relationship can thrive. Without self-awareness, self-respect, and self-discipline, every connection you have will mirror your internal chaos, insecurity, or emotional instability. The quality of your life truly depends on the quality of your relationships, and that starts with the one you have within.

I remember the day I realized my words were no longer mine—they were reactions.

I was sitting across from someone I loved, speaking with intensity, but underneath it, was fear.

Not love.

Not truth.

Just fear masquerading as communication.

I had meditated that morning, but I hadn't gone inward.

I had prayed, but I hadn't listened.

My words weren't rooted in me—they were echoes of my past wounds.

That was the moment I realized that you cannot communicate clearly if you are not clear within.

The reason my marriage failed was because I was failing.

And once I finally fixed my relationship with myself, it was too late.

I now know this is the number one problem in failed relationships and marriages: You cannot possibly hold loving space for another human if you don't hold yourself first.

At least one of the two people in the union must have the capacity to hold another until they are able to hold themselves—or else it will never work. You are setting yourself up for massive failure.

Relationships don't collapse from one big fight or one mistake. They deteriorate through subtle miscommunications and unmet emotional needs that slowly grow into silence, distance, and disconnection.

And communication? It is not about talking—it's about transmitting your truth clearly, calmly, and compassionately. But if you're not rooted in your truth, all you're doing is bleeding your pain onto someone else.

When I coach clients through relationship breakdowns, the question I always ask is, **"Are you speaking from fear, or are you speaking from love?"**

Fear speaks loudly. Fear blames. Fear avoids. Fear projects.

But love...love listens. Love stays. Love sees.

Clear, conscious communication begins with self-awareness.

You need to know:

- What you feel.
- Why you feel it.
- What you need.
- How to express it without attacking or abandoning it.

This is the true art of communication—and it begins long before you open your mouth.

Your ability to be in a healthy relationship is determined by how well you've learned to love, listen to, and lead yourself.

If you're in a partnership right now, ask yourself:

- *Do I feel safe expressing myself?*
- *Does my partner feel safe around me?*
- *Are we responding to or reacting to one another?*
- *Are we trying to be understood more than we're trying to understand?*

And if you're not in a relationship, ask:

- *Would I want to be in a relationship with someone like me?*
- *Do I give myself the kind of love, respect, and attention I desire from another?*

You cannot communicate clearly if you are not clear within.

Your words carry your frequency. Your presence is your power. Your wounds will speak louder than your intentions—unless you've done the inner work.

Before you engage in a difficult conversation, take five minutes to sit with yourself. Ask:

- *What am I feeling?*
- *What am I afraid of?*
- *What do I truly want?*

Get clear within yourself first, then speak. **Because the quality of your relationships will never exceed the quality of your relationship with yourself.**

The most transformational relationships begin not with finding the right partner but with becoming the right person. This chapter isn't about how to speak to others better or how to have fewer arguments. It's about cultivating the internal foundation required to communicate clearly, love freely, and stand firmly in truth.

You cannot give what you do not have. And so, if you seek peace, you must become peaceful. If you desire depth, you must become introspective. If you crave connection, you must connect with yourself first. It all begins and ends with you.

"Be impeccable with your word." — Don Miguel Ruiz

This principle is about so much more than just being honest. It's about being aligned. Speaking with intention. Refusing to say things you don't mean or make promises you won't keep. Being impeccable with your word begins with how you speak to yourself. If your inner dialogue is filled with shame, blame, and fear, it will eventually leak into how you treat others. But if your inner voice becomes a source of love, encouragement, and discipline, your external relationships will transform.

I've lived this. I've seen the difference in how I show up in conversations when I've done my morning prayer, my workout, journaled thoughts on paper, and made food choices in alignment with my values. That internal clarity allows you to communicate without confusion, to express emotion without dumping it on others, and to listen without needing to defend. Being impeccable with your word is a form of self-leadership.

> *"The quality of your life ultimately depends on*
> *the quality of your relationships."*
> — *Esther Perel*

These words cut to the core. No amount of money, success, or personal achievements can fulfill you if your relationships are in turmoil. But what most people miss is that your external relationships are just extensions of the relationship you have with yourself. It's not just about having better friends, a better partner, or a better support system. It's about being the kind of person who attracts and maintains healthy, loving, truth-filled relationships.

To do that, you have to forge yourself into someone who is capable of holding the life you desire. That means you can no longer run from pain. You must feel it, learn from it, and release it. It means you take responsibility for your patterns, your projections, and your part in every conflict. It means you develop rhythms in your life that reinforce self-trust—daily movement, deep rest, quiet reflection, spiritual alignment, clean fuel, and honest feedback loops.

When you build this kind of life from the inside out, you build a foundation that can hold anything you desire. You are no longer operating from fear or desperation but from vision and values. You are no longer trying to be loved; you are already loving. That shift changes everything.

I have felt this shift personally. When I fasted to clear my mind, to gain clarity, when I stopped eating for emotional reasons and began eating for performance and recovery—I created a version of myself that no longer needed external validation. That version of me is magnetic. Grounded. Clear.

And because of that, my communication became a superpower. My relationships improved because my energy within myself improved.

There is no limit to what you can achieve when you live in this level of alignment. The people you attract are different. The opportunities that arise are different. Even your ability to weather hard seasons changes. You become someone who can hold success, love, purpose, and pressure without breaking.

So yes, communication and relationships matter. But they must be built on a foundation of self-mastery. That's what this book offers you: a rhythm of living, a way of being that turns you into the kind of person who can hold everything you desire. And once you're there, there is no ceiling.

It all begins with you.

Let's get started cultivating the internal foundation required to communicate clearly, love freely, and stand firmly in your truth.

Each of these is a skill and a state of being that comes from internal alignment, not external performance. Here's how we'll do it, with practical steps and reflective practices for each area.

Communicate Clearly (With Yourself First)
Clarity comes from stillness and alignment.

Before you speak or express outwardly, you must be able to listen inwardly.

Daily Practices:

- **Journal Prompts**
  What do I need to express today that I haven't been saying?
  What am I avoiding communicating, and why?

- **Breath and Stillness Practice**
  Take three to five minutes in silence every morning—no phone, no music, just breath. Listen. Feel your energy. Notice where you're holding tension or anxiety. This creates the habit of tuning in first.

- **Speak Truth Over Yourself**
  Recite a daily truth:
  "I honor myself by telling the truth. I trust myself to say what needs to be said."

Reminder: Every time you lie to yourself (saying "I'm fine" when you're not or avoiding a conversation), it compounds into confusion. Clarity is the reward for honesty.

Love Freely (Without Fear, Control, or Expectations)

You can only love others to the depth you love yourself.

To love freely, you have to drop the need to be loved in return. That only happens when you feel secure within.

Daily Practices:

- **Mirror Work**
  Every morning or evening, stand in front of a mirror and say to yourself:
  "I love you. I'm proud of how far you've come."
  This sounds simple, but it forces you to face any discomfort with yourself.

- **Release Work**
  Write a letter to someone (don't send it) where you express love without needing anything back. It might start with:
  "I release the need for you to respond. I choose to love without control."

- **Check Your Motives**
  Before any relationship exchange, ask:
  "Am I trying to control the outcome here, or am I showing up in love?"

Reminder: Real love doesn't grasp, manipulate, or cling. The freer your love, the more powerful it becomes.

Stand Firmly in Your Truth (Unapologetically and Humbly)
Your truth is your responsibility. No one can live it for you.

Standing in your truth requires you to know what you value, what you believe, and what you're unwilling to compromise.

Daily Practices:

- **Journal Prompts**
  Where in my life am I shrinking to fit in or be liked?
  What truth am I afraid to tell, and what would change if I said it?

- **Core Values Check-In**
  Write down your top three values. For one week, ask yourself every day:
  Did my actions align with these today?

- **Truth-Telling Practice**
  Practice saying hard truths in low-stakes situations (e.g., "I'm not available," "That doesn't work for me," or "Here's what I need."). Build the muscle of honest expression.

Reminder: Truth-telling isn't about being loud or right. It's about being rooted in who you are. That energy is unshakable.

Integration: Build the Foundation with Daily Rhythm

Here's a simple rhythm to integrate all three elements into your day:

Morning

- Breath and prayer (5–10 minutes)
- Journal one question from above
- Mirror work (two minutes)

Afternoon

- Values check-in
- Lovingly express a truth (text, voice note, or conversation)

Evening

- Reflect:
  Did I speak clearly today?
  Did I love freely today?
  Did I stay true to myself?

This practice is about bringing even more consciousness and consistency to your internal dialogue. When you live in integrity with yourself, your communication becomes clean, your love becomes unconditional, and your truth becomes magnetic.

The Fast Track to Authentic Connection

Most people, including my survival self, try to improve their relationships by fixing what's *external*—communication tactics, boundary scripts, attachment styles. But true, lasting harmony with others begins with something much deeper: radical self-honesty.

And there is no greater tool I have found for initiating this transformation than fasting.

Especially at the seventy-two-hour mark of a water fast, a profound shift occurs. You begin to meet yourself, not the self who performs for the world, not the self reacting out of wounding or habit, but the *real* self. The one who emerges after you've denied the body, silenced the noise, and sat still long enough to peel back the layers of ego, identity, fear, and old programming.

Fasting forces presence. It strips away distractions. It reveals where you reach for comfort instead of truth. It places you in front of your own fire and invites you to stand still—not to escape, not to numb, but to feel. And in that fire, you're refined.

By the time you cross that threshold—when the hunger fades and clarity arises—you're no longer who you were when you began. You've shed the masks. The lies you told yourself. The attachments that dulled your frequency. You don't want the same things anymore. You don't crave the same validation, the same drama, the same shallow connections. You become less reactive. More reverent. You begin to *see* others because you've finally seen yourself.

From this space of inner sovereignty, your relationships change—not because other people change, but because *you* do.

You're no longer looking for people to fill your emptiness. You're no longer defending a version of yourself that isn't real. You're no longer engaging from woundedness or insecurity. You are home within yourself. And from that place, your communication is clearer. Your love is purer. Your presence is more magnetic.

This is why fasting is not just a health practice—it's a communication practice. It sharpens your internal dialogue so you can better relate to the world outside of you. Because if you cannot sit with your own emotions, you will not hold space for someone else's. If you cannot hear the truth in your own heart, you will not speak truth in your relationships.

Self-mastery is the highest form of love. And fasting is the sacred tool that invites you there.

So if you want better relationships—start with a fast. Not to punish yourself. Not to "lose weight." But to *meet yourself*. To reclaim your authority. To align with the frequency of truth.

Because when you live unmasked, you love unmasked. And that is where real connection begins.

CHAPTER 7

EXERCISE & MOVEMENT

"Train the body to strengthen the mind."
– Mar Morabito

Most people treat movement like a chore. I treat it like a ceremony.

This isn't about chasing aesthetics. This isn't about looking good naked. This is about clarity. This is about energy. This is about choosing sovereignty in motion.

Movement, to me, is prayer. It's discipline. Its momentum becomes physical. It's how I stay sane, sharp, spiritually aligned, and emotionally grounded.

I don't train because I want to lose weight. I train because I want to think clearly. I want to *feel God ignite me*. I want to move stagnant emotions out of my body and get back to that still, clear place where I *know* who I am.

The Science: Training the Body to Train the Brain

When you move, your physiology changes. When your physiology changes, your emotions follow. When your emotions shift, your thoughts get clearer. That's not just spiritual—it's neurological.

Movement does three things:

1. Increases brain-derived neurotrophic factor, or BDNF—a growth hormone for your brain.
2. Boosts dopamine and serotonin, neurotransmitters responsible for motivation, reward, and mood regulation.
3. Improves insulin sensitivity and reduces inflammation, which impacts your focus, recovery, and long-term resilience.

HRV: The Nervous System Doesn't Lie

I've tracked every run, every walk, every bike ride, and every training block for over seven years using WHOOP. The truth? When I'm *moving*, my HRV rises. When I stop, stagnate, get lazy, or emotional, my metrics tank.

This isn't about breaking a sweat. It's about regulating my nervous system and building emotional durability through physical discipline.

Your WHOOP score is just a reflection of how honest you're being with your body. Mine doesn't lie. It tells me exactly how aligned I am—or am not.

Movement equals energy management.

Everything is energy. When you move your body, you move energy. When you stay still, stagnant, and spiral mentally, you clog the system.

I use movement to process.

Rage? I sprint.

Sadness? I walk.

Confusion? I bike.

Frustration? I hit the floor and rep it out.

This is how I transmute chaos into clarity—not by suppressing it but by sweating through it.

The Ritual: Resilience Through Rhythm

This is what I call my **Movement Trinity**—the three non-negotiables that keep me aligned daily:

1. **Sweat**: Run, bike, weighted vest.
2. **Strength**: Pushups, squats, air work, isometrics.
3. **Stillness**: Backbends, breathwork, walks with my dog.

Every day, I move with intention—not for calories, but for clarity.

What Happens When I Don't Move

When I skip movement, I feel it in every layer of my being:

- My HRV drops.
- Max VO2 drops.
- My irritability increases.
- My emotions feel louder, heavier, and less manageable.
- My thoughts spiral faster and sharper.

Movement isn't optional. It's medicine. It's a prescription I fill daily without fail.

Resentment can't live in a body that sweats out its stories daily.

Why Movement Is Sovereignty

To live sovereignly means to be in control of your emotional state, and that starts in your body. You can't think clearly when your nervous system is hijacked. And your nervous system doesn't care about your to-do list. It listens to your body's rhythm.

If I'm not moving, I'm not leading. Period.

Leadership starts with energetic mastery. You cannot pour clean energy into others if you are blocked, stagnant, or inflamed. Movement clears the channel.

Rewire Through Movement: A Practical Framework

1. **Morning momentum:** Pushups, air squats, backbends, and walks with Pearly anchor my day in execution, not emotion.

2. **Fasted cardio:** A forty- to ninety-minute run or weighted walk keeps my mind sharp and my body metabolically flexible.

3. **Evening flow:** A sunset walk, gentle stretch, or breathwork releases the day from my nervous system and closes the loop.

Energetic Truth: Movement As Medicine

We live in a hyper-dopaminergic world—too much stimulation, not enough sensation. Movement brings us back into the body. Into sensation. Into now.

The word *emotion* literally means "energy in motion." So if you don't move it, you *store* it—in your tissues, joints, organs, and breath. It becomes tension, inflammation, and trauma.

But when you move intentionally, you're clearing that emotion like a storm system.

You can't cry it out, journal it out, or talk it out unless you've first sweat it out.

Reflection + Action Workbook for Sovereign Training

Journal Prompts:

1. *When do I feel most clear—before or after I move?*

2. *What emotion tends to block me from training consistently?*

3. *What movement am I avoiding that my body is begging for?*

Challenge:

→ Seven-Day Movement Trinity

- Each day, complete your version of:
  - One sweat session
  - One strength ritual
  - One walk or stretch

→ Track your mood and HRV. Journal the shift.

You are not tired. You are uninspired. Move.

You are not broken. You are stagnant. Move.

You are not confused. You are clogged. Move.

When you honor your body, you create the clarity required to lead your mind and spirit.

This is how I stay sovereign—one rep, one step, one breath at a time.

CHAPTER 8

GOAL SETTING & PLANNING

"Turn vision into direction. A sovereign life is built with intention.
Every action becomes an arrow aimed at your higher self."
– Mar Morabito

I used to write goals on a whiteboard and call it vision.
I used to buy planners, write big dreams in all caps, highlight them, circle them—then forget them.

Because writing it down isn't the work.
Living it out is.

Sovereignty doesn't come from setting goals. It comes from living with structure.
Structure is safety. Structure is clarity. Structure is where freedom lives.

This chapter is about aiming your actions like arrows so every step you take leads toward the highest version of you. Not who the world expects. Not who your old patterns crave. But the one who knows where they're going.

The Truth About Goal Setting: Most People Set Goals From Ego, Not Identity

The world says, "set SMART goals."
I say start with your self-concept. Who are you becoming? That's where your real goals live.

A sovereign doesn't ask: *What do I want?*
A sovereign asks: *What do I need to do daily to become who I'm called to be?*

That's the difference between *ambition* and *alignment*.

This isn't about getting more done.
It's about getting clearer.

The Psychology of Direction: Why Your Brain Needs Targets

Your brain is a prediction machine. It doesn't want chaos—it wants clarity. When you don't give it direction, it creates noise. Anxiety. Overthinking. Distraction.

Clear goals *calm the mind*. They give the nervous system something to organize around. They direct your energy and eliminate decision fatigue.

When I have a target:

- My cravings fade.
- My anger dissipates.
- My emotional noise gets quieter.
- My HRV holds steady. I sleep more deeply. I move sharply.

Because *direction is regulation*. And regulation is how you stay sovereign.

Three-Layer Goal Framework: Spirit—Body—Mind

I break my goals into three domains:

1. Spirit (Being)

→ Who do I need to *become* to hold the life I'm building?
→ What are my non-negotiables that shape my energy, values, and faith?

Example:

- Journal and pray every morning.
- No phone until after God, breathwork, and a run.
- Live by standards, not feelings.

2. Body (Doing)

→ What does my routine look like to embody that identity?
→ What movement, fasting, or rituals ground me in discipline?

Example:

- Fast 16:8 daily.
- Run five times per week.
- Do one hundred pushups, squats, and mountain climbers daily.
- Go to sleep by 10 p.m. Wake up by 6 a.m. Walk Pearly each morning and evening.

3. Mind (Having)

→ What do I want to build, create, or earn as the outcome of my embodiment?
→ What is measurable and trackable?

Example:

- Publish *Survival to Sovereignty*.

- Launch a ninety-day coaching sprint with ten high-ticket clients.
- Save $[X] by September.

Note: *It's not vision boards and vibes. It's math and momentum.*

From Vision to System: My Real-Life Planning Strategy

Every Sunday, I run what I call the Sovereign Strategy Session.

Here's the exact flow:

1. Review the Data

- WHOOP metrics: HRV, recovery, strain, and sleep.
- *Did my actions last week align with my goals?*
- *How did I feel? Where did I spiral? What needs to be eliminated?*

2. Reconnect to the Why

- *Who do I want to be by the end of this quarter?*
- *What habits will make that inevitable?*

3. Recalibrate My Week

- I plug in my non-negotiables first: runs, fasts, training, and journaling.
- Then, I schedule high-value priorities: writing, content creation, and coaching calls.
- Then, and only then, I allow for flexibility: errands, meetings, and downtime.

If it's not on the calendar, it's not real.

Why Planning Isn't Restriction—It's Leadership

You don't create a powerful life by winging it.

Every action is either taking you closer to your vision or back to your old self.

When you plan with intention:

- Your nervous system calms.
- Your self-trust deepens.
- Your cravings disappear.
- Your results compound.

Planning is not about controlling the outcome. It's about owning the input.

Rewire With Planning: A Practical Framework

Your Daily Non-Negotiables

- Choose three to five habits that anchor your identity. Do them *regardless* of how you feel.

Examples might include fasting until noon, running at sunrise, journaling and praying, and taking magnesium nightly.

→ These are not optional. These are your anchors.

Weekly Sovereign Strategy Session

- Every Sunday, sit down with your calendar and plan around:
  - Spirit: time with God, stillness, solitude
  - Body: training, fasting, movement
  - Mind: business, content, money, mastery

→ Plan the week as the person you're becoming, not as the person you've been.

Reflection + Action Workbook for Goal Setting & Planning

1. Identity-Based Goal Setting:
- *Who do I need to become?*
- *What daily action proves I'm becoming that person?*

2. Goal Breakdown (Spirit/Body/Mind):
- Choose one measurable goal in each category.
- Break it into weekly actions.

3. Create Your "Sovereign 5":
- Five daily actions that make you feel like *you're in charge.*

4. Weekly Journal Prompts:
- *What worked?*
- *What distracted me?*
- *What did my data say?*
- *What would the next level version of me shift?*

Planning is a spiritual act. It says: "I'm not waiting on the world to change. I'm becoming the person who can build it."

If you keep waking up and hoping the day goes differently, you're still a slave to emotion. A sovereign wakes up and *decides* how the day will go.

You are the arrow.
You are the archer.
You are the target.

So draw the bow. Aim with intention. And shoot.

CHAPTER 9

SOVEREIGN STANDARDS: CREATING THE NEW YOU

"Your identity is upheld by your standards—not your circumstances."
– Mar Morabito

Everyone talks about discipline.
Everyone talks about goals.
But here's what no one tells you:

Your life is not built by what you say you want.
It's built by the standard you refuse to fall beneath *on the days you don't feel like it*.

This is where self-mastery becomes embodiment.
This is the transition from practice to presence.
This is where the rhythms stop being a checklist and start becoming your code.

Standards Over Circumstances

You don't become sovereign because life got easier. You become sovereign because you chose yourself even when it didn't feel good.
Even when you were tired.
Even when you were triggered.
Even when your metrics were red and your motivation was low.

"Sovereignty begins when your word becomes your law." — Mar Morabito

Standards are not rules. They are rhythms. They're who you *are*, not what you *try to do.*

The Sovereign Equation: Identity = Standards x Repetition

Let me be clear: Your life is not the result of motivation. It's not the result of hacks, hustle, or hustle culture. It's the result of *energetic integrity.*

That means what you do when no one's watching. That means how you act when your routine gets tested. That means how you reset when life gets loud.

This is about building your *Rule of Life.*

The Rule of Life Framework: Rhythm as Your Foundation

Your sovereign self doesn't arise from chaos. It's built through rhythm. Not rigidity. Not perfection. Rhythm.

Here's how I build mine:

Morning: Anchor

> *"The way you start your day is the way you shape your life."*
> *— Mar Morabito*

I don't react. I lead. From the *moment* I wake up.

My Sovereign Morning Architecture:

- Wake up when my body is recovered.
- Take morning supplement stack.
- Workout in a fasted state.
- Pray and journal.
- Get silent.

This isn't about a vibe. It's about *vitality*. Because how you start the day is the blueprint for how you handle stress, temptation, and resistance later on.

Midday: Execution

> *"Energy management > time management."*
> — *Mar Morabito*

Midday is not a time to coast—it's where my *action matches my intention*.

Midday Standards:

- Work on high-focus priorities.
- Complete coaching or client meetings.
- No distractions, no dopamine loops, no food-based energy crashes.
- Go on a walk or another form of movement to recalibrate at 1.5x pace.
- Stick to a clean eating window: keto, high-fat, low-carb, plant-based, protein priority.

I don't leave this to chance. I *architect* my midday around sovereignty, not survival.

Evening: Integration

> *"If your nighttime is chaos, your next morning is already lost."*
> — *Mar Morabito*

Evening is where I close the loop. Where I return to presence. Where I *protect the temple*—my sleep, my recovery, my peace.

Evening Sovereign Rituals:

- Walk Pearly at sunset.
- Move my body if I feel energy needs releasing beyond a walk.
- No food after a certain time.
- No screens one hour before bed.
- Take magnesium and evening supplements.
- Shower, stretch, read, journal, and reflect.

Because here's the truth:

> *Your next level doesn't come from pushing harder.*
> *It comes from resting deeper, planning sharper, and honoring your standards like they're sacred.*

From Routine to Identity

This is where most people fail.
They chase routines, but they never internalize identity.

You can't act like a sovereign once a week and expect to live in alignment.
This is about rehearsing your future self in real time—every single day.

The rituals are there to support your standards.
Your standards exist to uphold your identity.

If it's not embodied, it's empty.

Sovereign Standards:

1. Identify your current baseline standard.
→ What is your *minimum* standard for food, movement, prayer, recovery, and business?

2. Now, define your next level standard.
→ What does your highest self demand of you, daily?

3. Create your non-negotiable rhythm:
- Morning Anchor:
- Midday Execution:
- Evening Integration:

4. Ask: What breaks this rhythm?
→ Is it emotion? Is it distraction? Is it doubt?

5. Commit to realignment.
→ Sovereignty is not perfection—it's *recalibration*.

This is where the seven rhythms stop being isolated ideas and start becoming an integrated life.

Fasting? It only works when you hold the line.
Prayer? It only connects when your day isn't chaotic.
Sleep? It only restores you when you honor your evenings.
Movement? It only energizes you when it's daily.
Nutrition? It only aligns when it's not just physical, but spiritual.
Communication? It only deepens when you're regulated.
Goals? They only land when your system supports your soul.

All of it—every part of it—is upheld by your standards.

Be Undeniable

You don't need more effort. You need *alignment.*
You don't need to prove your worth. You need to *honor your word.*
You don't need to try harder. You need to *remember who the f*ck you are.*

This chapter is the gateway from practice to embodiment.
From chasing results to embodying truth.
From doing more to *being* more.

You're not building a better to-do list.
You're building a rule of life so consistent, so honest, and so clean that even on your worst day, you're still dangerous.

CHAPTER 10

THE RESET: SLAYING THE OLD SELF

"You don't just become new—you have to bury what kept you broken."
– Mar Morabito

You're not crazy.

You're just coming face to face with the old you, and it doesn't want to die quietly.

This is the part where most people fold. They go back to the addiction. The excuses. The drama. The food. The porn. The laziness. The relationship they know isn't for them. The life that's too small but feels safe.

Why?

Because transformation has a cost.
And the price is always the same: *your old identity.*

The Comfort Creep

You've had a perfect week. Your metrics are dialed. You're eating clean. You're moving with purpose. Your prayer time is rich. You feel unstoppable.

And then out of nowhere, you skip your fast. You miss your run. You eat the thing. You text the ex. You scroll till 2 a.m. You just stop showing up.

Welcome to the war.

This is the resistance and your reset. And it's not random—it's *ritual*.
The final test before you step into the next level of you.

> *"The closer you get to the promise, the louder your patterns will scream."*
> — *Mar Morabito*

The Spiritual Warfare Behind Your Relapse

This isn't just mental.
This is spiritual. This is war.

> *"The thief comes only to steal and kill and destroy..."*
> *(John 10:10)*

Every craving, every emotional spiral, every old pattern that whispers, *"...just once won't hurt"*—that's not just weakness. That's warfare.

And the devil doesn't need to destroy you.
He just needs to distract you.
He just needs to get you to *break your word to yourself.*

Because once you break that, you start questioning everything else.

The Old You Doesn't Die in Silence

Let's be honest.

There's a version of you that loves chaos.
That version *thrives* in the familiar.
It loves the dopamine of self-sabotage.
It loves the drama of pretending you're healing while still holding on to the habits that keep you sick.

"The old you isn't going to surrender without a fight. You have to kill it."
— *Mar Morabito*

And killing it doesn't mean perfection.
It means no longer negotiating with it.

The Loop: Relapse → Shame → Sabotage

Here's how the enemy plays it:

1. **Temptation**: "You've done so well, you deserve this."
2. **Justification**: "It's not that big of a deal."
3. **Collapse**: "F*ck it. I already messed up—what's one more?"
4. **Shame**: "Why do I always do this?"
5. **Avoidance**: "I'll start again next week."
6. **Repeat**.

This isn't about the food. Or the phone. Or the ex.
This is about identity. You still think you're the person who breaks promises.

Reclaiming Your Word to Yourself

When I was in my lowest spiral, it wasn't the pain that broke me. It was the *disappointment*. The shame of knowing I wasn't living up to my own standards. The *guilt* of knowing what I was capable of and choosing less anyway.

But you don't need to be perfect to walk in power.

You just need to make **your word law again**.

Not *sometimes*.

Not *when it feels good*.

But *every* time.

Because when your word becomes non-negotiable, *you become untouchable.*

The Inner Battleground Map

You need to know what you're up against. Map it. Name it. Drag it into the light.

1. Your Triggers
→ What moments, foods, people, and patterns pull you back?
Write them down. Build guardrails.

2. Your Weapons
→ Fasting. Cold showers. Prayer. Running. Journaling. Walking. Worship.
Keep them sharp. Use them *before* the breakdown.

3. Your Signal
→ Know the feeling in your body before you spiral.
Tight chest? Shaky hands? Irritation? Apathy?
That's your body warning you. Don't ignore it.

4. Your Truth
→ Write your truth as a weapon.
"I am not my cravings."
"I am not going back."
"I am not here to be entertained — I'm here to be transformed."

Slay the Old Self:

1. What behavior keeps creeping back in when you're uncomfortable?
→ Write it. Face it. Name it.

2. What truth do you need to speak over it?
→ "That's not who I am anymore."

3. What's one thing you can do daily that proves that version of you is gone?
→ Fast. Move. Speak truth. Take the walk instead of the scroll.

4. When you fall, how fast do you return?
→ That's the real flex. Not perfection—*recalibration.*

You Have to Decide Who Dies

Here's what no one tells you:

You don't need more healing. You need more honesty.
You don't need another thirty-day challenge. You need to *kill the thing keeping you average.*
You don't need motivation. You need a funeral.

Decide who dies.

The version of you who lies to herself or himself?
Or the version of you who finally walks in truth?
Because only one gets to live.

CHAPTER 11

COMMANDING THE FIELD
THE RETURN: LIVING IN FLOW, FULLY YOU

"Sovereignty isn't a mountaintop. It's a rhythm."
– Mar Morabito

You've done the work. You've burned the bridges. You've buried the old you. Now what?

Now, you *return.*

Not to who you were.
Not to the world you came from.
But to who you were always meant to be.

This is the part no one talks about: *What happens after the breakthrough?*
After the fast. After the discipline. After the rewiring, the awakening, the slaying.

You return home.
Fully you.
Unapologetically alive.

Flow Is Not a Feeling—It's a Frequency

Everyone thinks "flow" is some magical state you fall into when the stars align.
It's not. Flow is what happens when *you stop lying to yourself.*

When you stop breaking your word.
When your body, mind, and spirit are finally on the same page.
When your actions match your truth.

Flow is a byproduct of rhythm.
And rhythm is the result of *repetition and reverence.*

Integration > Obsession

Let me make something clear:

Obsession is emotional.
Integration is energetic.

Obsession burns hot and fast. Integration *sustains.*

You don't need to be militant forever. But you do need to stay in rhythm.

This book isn't about forcing you to become someone else. It's about walking you back to yourself.
Not the performative you. Not the addicted you. Not the reactive you.

The *aligned* you.
The *embodied* you.
The one who leads without speaking and impacts without pushing.

That's real leadership. That's sovereignty.

Becoming the Mirror

When you live like this, something wild happens:
You stop having to explain yourself.

People *feel* you.
They feel your energy when you walk into a room.
They feel your clarity, your alignment, your stillness.

You become the mirror that forces others to confront their own chaos.
You don't have to preach. You just have to *be*.

> *Your life becomes the evidence.*
> *Your consistency becomes the testimony.*

That's why your sovereignty isn't just about you. It's your *assignment*.
The world doesn't need more noise. It needs more *embodied examples*.

The Return: A 30-Day Sovereign Rhythm Map

Here's how to *live this* now, not someday.
You've learned the rhythms. Now you *walk them out*.

Daily Non-Negotiables

- Fast until at least noon.
- Run, walk, or train your body.
- Journal and pray before using your phone.
- Fuel your body with plant-based keto meals or whatever works best for you.
- Go on a walk at sunrise and sunset with presence.
- Go to bed by 10 p.m. after you've taken magnesium and practiced stillness.

You don't need to do all of it. You just need to do what *grounds* you. Every day. No matter what.

Weekly Strategy Session (Every Sunday)

- Review your rhythms and WHOOP data.
- Reconnect with your higher self: *Who am I becoming?*
- Schedule in rhythms first, then let the rest fall around them.
- Reflect on how you felt, not just what you achieved
- Clean up your language, choices, inputs, and intentions.

Reflection Prompts (Weekly)

- *Where did I lead with truth this week?*
- *Where did I regress into comfort or performance?*
- *What needs to be cut, simplified, or recommitted to?*
- *What am I pretending not to see or feel?*

You don't need another plan.
You don't need another guru.
You don't need another restart.

You just need to *remember* who you are, why you're here, and what promises you make to yourself when no one is watching.

This isn't the end of a book.
It's the beginning of your return.

Now walk.
In rhythm.
In truth.
In flow.
In power.
In God.

THE SOVEREIGN DECLARATION

God, I no longer run. I return.
I return to who You created me to be—whole, aligned, and awake.
I release the versions of me that were built in fear, pain, and performance.
I bury the chaos. I bury the addiction. I bury the lie that I am not enough.
I step into my assignment, fully surrendered, fully me.

Let my life be evidence of Your grace.
Let my discipline be worship.
Let my body be a temple.
Let my rhythm be my testimony.

I choose to live sovereign—not someday, but *now.*
Not for perfection, but for presence.
Not for applause, but for alignment.

God, use me. Move through me. Live in me.
I am Yours. I am home.
Amen.

Welcome home.

BONUS MATERIALS + APPENDIX

The Sovereign Stride: A 30-Day Challenge to Return to You

This isn't a challenge for the sake of a challenge.
This is a mirror. A rhythm. A return.
Thirty days to walk in sovereignty—not perfectly, but consistently.
You don't need more hacks. You need more *honesty*.

The Sovereign Stride: 30-Day Challenge Overview
The Mission

To live the rhythms. To embody the standard. To track your truth.

One day at a time. For thirty days.

How It Works

- **Daily Rituals**: Simple non-negotiables done consistently.
- **Weekly Reflections**: Journaling prompts that reveal where you're hiding.
- **Data Awareness**: Tracking metrics that *don't lie*.
- **Faith Integration**: Scriptures to anchor you in truth.
- **Made-Up Mind Declaration**: A written vow to yourself that you revisit daily.

DAILY RHYTHM PROMPTS

- *Wake time?*
- *How many hours did I sleep?*
- *How many steps did I walk?*
- *How many calories did I consume?*
- *How many calories did I expend?*
- *How many hours did I fast?*
- *Did I work out?*
- *What is my HRV?*
- *Mood (1-5)*
- *Win of the day*

WEEKLY JOURNAL PROMPTS

WEEK 1: Awareness

- *What did I notice about my patterns this week?*
- *What distractions am I still letting win?*
- *What truth did I avoid speaking to myself?*

WEEK 2: Alignment

- *What rhythms felt most natural? Which felt forced?*
- *Where did I feel God's presence strongest?*
- *What is He asking me to lie down?*

WEEK 3: Ownership

- *Where did I break my word? Why?*
- *What can no longer travel with me into this next chapter?*
- *How am I using movement to move through emotion?*

WEEK 4: Embodiment

- *What's different about me now versus thirty days ago?*
- *What standard am I no longer available to fall beneath?*
- *What am I ready to teach, lead, or share from this?*

Sovereign Self-Assessment Questions
1. Self-Trust Scale (Rate 1–5)

- I keep the promises I make to myself.
- I show up when I say I will, even when I don't feel like it.
- I know what foods help me feel aligned.

- I know how to return to rhythm quickly.
- I track my truth (sleep, movement, intake, emotions).

Score 20–25 → Sovereign

Score 10–19 → In progress

Score 1–9 → Audit your inputs and rebuild trust.

QUICK-REFERENCE
SOVEREIGN CHEAT SHEET

Rhythm	What to Track	Tools
Fasting & TRE	Hours Fasted	Zero, WHOOP, Journal
Prayer & Meditation	Time spent/feeling after	Timer, Bible App, Dr. Joe Dispenza
Sleep & Recovery	Hours slept, REM %, HRV	WHOOP, Oura
Nutrition	Food type, calories, macros	MyFitnessPal, Photo Log
Movement	Steps, cardio zone, training	WHOOP Strain, Apple Watch
Communication	Conflict avoided or resolved?	Journal
Planning	Did I plan my day/week?	Calendar, Notion, Planner

Scripture Index by Rhythm

Fasting & Self-Control

- *Matthew 4:4*: "Man shall not live on bread alone..."
- *Galatians 5:22–23*: "...self-control."

Prayer & Meditation

- *1 Thessalonians 5:17*: "Pray without ceasing."
- *Psalm 46:10*: "Be still and know that I am God."

Sleep & Recovery

- *Psalm 127:2*: "...He gives His beloved sleep."
- *Ecclesiastes 3:1*: "There is a time to rest..."

Nutrition

- *1 Corinthians 10:31*: "Whether you eat or drink...do it all to the glory of God."
- *Proverbs 25:27*: "It is not good to eat too much honey..."

Movement

- *1 Corinthians 6:19–20*: "Your body is a temple..."
- *Isaiah 40:31*: "They shall run and not grow weary."

Communication & Relationships

- *Proverbs 15:1*: "A gentle answer turns away wrath..."
- *Ephesians 4:29*: "Let no corrupt talk come out of your mouth..."

Discipline & Planning

- *Proverbs 21:5*: "The plans of the diligent lead to abundance."
- *Habakkuk 2:2*: "Write the vision. Make it plain."

MADE-UP MIND
DECLARATION TEMPLATE

I, _____, have made up my mind to walk in sovereignty.

I will no longer betray myself.

I will honor the rhythms God has revealed to me.

I will fast when I don't want to.

I will speak the truth when it's uncomfortable.

I will rest when my body calls for it.

I will train when my mind wants to retreat.

I will nourish my temple, not numb it.

I will lead myself with reverence, not rules.

My mind is made up.

My rhythms are set.

I am not here to fit in—I am here to be free.

From this day forward, I walk as the one God created me to be.

Not perfectly. But honestly.

Not someday. But now.

→ **Sign it. Read it every day for the next thirty days. Then live it.**

RECOMMENDED RESOURCES & INFLUENCERS

Below is a list of individuals and works that helped shape my journey from survival mode into embodied sovereignty.

Fasting, Metabolic Healing, & Nutrition

Dr. Jason Fung

- **Notable Work**: *The Obesity Code, The Complete Guide to Fasting*
- **Role**: Nephrologist and leading authority on intermittent fasting and insulin resistance
- **Impact**: His phrase "hunger is the teacher" became a spiritual anchor for my fasting journey. His work demystified the science of fasting and helped me reclaim my body.

Dr. Mindy Pelz

- **Notable Work**: *Fast Like a Girl*
- **Role**: Women's fasting expert focused on cycle syncing and hormone healing
- **Impact**: Reinforced my understanding of the connection between fasting, female biology, and sovereign self-regulation.

Ben Azadi

- **Notable Work**: *Keto Flex, The Intermittent Fasting Cheat Sheet*
- **Role**: Founder of Keto Kamp, metabolic health expert

- **Impact:** Inspired me to embrace a clean, plant-based ketogenic lifestyle without shame or confusion. He simplified the science and helped me stay in the fire.

Dr. Will Cole

- **Notable Work:** *Ketotarian, Gut Feelings, The Inflammation Spectrum*
- **Role:** Functional medicine practitioner bridging keto and plant-based healing
- **Impact:** Helped me trust that plant-based keto was not only possible, but optimal for my body, my emotions, and my energetic alignment. Once the WHOOP data showed me real-time metrics accuracy, I knew I was on the right track.

Spirituality, Faith & Emotional Healing

Joyce Meyer

- **Notable Work:** *Battlefield of the Mind, The Confident Woman*
- **Role:** Christian teacher and author
- **Impact:** Source of biblical truth and spiritual strength during emotional battles, especially when I needed to re-anchor my identity and calm my mental warfare.

Aubrey Marcus

- **Notable Work:** *Own the Day, Own Your Life*
- **Role:** Human optimization leader, founder of Onnit
- **Impact:** Echoed my beliefs on daily rhythm, sovereignty, and ritualized discipline and provided a mirror for full-spectrum personal mastery. I have been transformed by him personally and his supplement line, Korrect Energy. After the first day of taking it, I pulled the trigger to invest in myself and decided to write this book. My consciousness told me it was time, and I listened without any

hesitation. In the past, I would have tried to negotiate, but I surrendered to the truth. I knew this supplement was sent for me to kickstart my God-given mission.

Dr. Joe Dispenza

- **Notable Work**: *Becoming Supernatural, Breaking the Habit of Being Yourself*
- **Role**: Neuroscientist and spiritual teacher
- **Impact**: Reinforced my understanding that identity is reprogrammed through repetition, meditation, and energy, not just willpower. He forever changed my life and paradigm.

Muscle, Protein, and the New Paradigm of Strength

Dr. Gabrielle Lyon

- **Notable Work**: *Forever Strong*
- **Role**: Creator of "Muscle-Centric Medicine"
- **Impact**: Taught me that muscle is the organ of longevity and that strength is a spiritual frequency, not just a physical one. Her work gave me the conviction to prioritize protein and train like a sovereign being. If it wasn't for her insight on creating a strong musculoskeletal system, I wouldn't be alive today. The doctors told me, when my ten-day-old appendix ruptured, that the only thing that saved me was my abdominal muscles holding the infection in like a band-aid.

Human Performance, Resilience, & Self-Mastery

David Goggins

- **Notable Work**: *Can't Hurt Me, Never Finished*
- **Role**: Ultra-endurance athlete, Navy SEAL, mental toughness coach

- **Impact**: Helped fuel my own banshee-level energy in survival mode—and my refusal to make excuses. I train like a soldier every day because for me, it is war, and my life depends on me showing up and showing myself who is the boss. No bell taps around here.

Andrew Huberman, Ph.D

- **Platform**: *Huberman Lab Podcast*
- **Role**: Neuroscientist at Stanford University
- **Impact**: Taught me the neuroscience behind behavior change, dopamine cycles, fasting, and sleep, making my lifestyle both sustainable and science-backed.

Gary Brecka

- **Notable Work**: *10X Health, Functional Biologist*
- **Role**: Human biologist & founder of The Ultimate Human
- **Impact**: Gary's breakdown of how "we don't have an energy problem, we have a mitochondrial problem" was the realization I needed when I saw the data for my workouts. My zones had changed when my mitochondria did. My cells were getting slowed down by the foods I was consuming. He gave language to what I had lived through—and backed the data I saw. He helped me biologically reclaim my power.

Dr. Casey Means

- **Notable Work**: *Good Energy*
- **Role**: Founder of Levels, metabolic health expert
- **Impact**: Reinforced my commitment to blood sugar regulation, cellular energy, and aligning my food choices with emotional and metabolic clarity.

Rich Roll

- **Notable Work**: *Finding Ultra, The Rich Roll Podcast*
- **Role**: Endurance athlete, bestselling author, plant-based wellness advocate
- **Impact**: Modeled the power of plant-based living, long-form introspection, and the spiritual depth that comes from endurance, solitude, and radical lifestyle change. Reinforced my belief in sovereignty through discipline and alignment.

Gut, Hormones & Plant-Based Living

Viome

- **Platform**: Personalized gut and health intelligence
- **Role**: Functional health testing company
- **Impact**: Helped me understand food as frequency, not just fuel— guiding my detox decisions, superfood choices, and plant-based protocol based on what my gut needed and wanted, not what I thought it did.

Dr. Neal Barnard

- **Notable Work**: *Your Body in Balance, Power Foods for the Brain*
- **Role**: Plant-based physician focused on hormones and brain health
- **Impact**: Helped me eliminate animal products with confidence by connecting diet to hormonal and emotional regulation.

Dr. Alan Goldhamer

- **Notable Work**: *The Pleasure Trap*
- **Role**: Water fasting expert and founder of TrueNorth Health
- **Impact**: Validated the power of longer fasts to reset the brain-body system and escape the addictive food trap.

Communication, Energy, & Nervous System Regulation

Gabor Maté

- **Notable Work**: *When the Body Says No, The Myth of Normal*
- **Role**: Addiction and trauma expert
- **Impact**: Offered me language to understand the connection between emotional stress, trauma, and chronic illness, and how to challenge the conventional understanding of health and disease.

Steven Pressfield

- **Notable Work**: *The War of Art*
- **Role**: Author and creative resistance expert
- **Impact**: Helped me name "resistance" as a real force and gave me the tools to beat it with ritual and rhythm, especially when writing this book.

TRACKING TOOL
I USE FOR SOVEREIGNTY

WHOOP

- **Platform**: Performance and recovery wearable
- **Impact**: I have worn WHOOP for over seven years and will never go a day without it. It has become my accountability tool and truth-teller, showing me how sleep, food, training, and emotion all impact my recovery, HRV, and alignment.

CLOSING REFLECTION

These are not just names I admire. These are the mentors, messengers, and methodologies that shaped my rebirth. Each one mirrored back a different piece of my truth. They didn't "save" me—I had to do that myself—but they illuminated the path.

Now I pass the torch to you.

Use these tools. Learn from these leaders. But more than anything, use your life as the ultimate lab. Your *sovereignty* will be earned, not given.

THANK YOU FOR READING MY BOOK!

To support your journey, I've created a FREE Portal & Community filled with tools, videos, and resources to keep you connected and accountable as you integrate this work into your life.

Scan the QR Code below and use the password: BOOK to enter.

I appreciate your interest in my book and value your feedback, as it helps me improve future versions. I would appreciate it if you could leave your invaluable review on Amazon.com with your feedback. Thank you!

www.ingramcontent.com/pod-product-compliance
Lightning Source LLC
Chambersburg PA
CBHW070044100426
42740CB00013B/2785